EPIC STORIES FOR KIDS AND FAMILIES

ACCIDENTAL DISCOVERIES THAT CHANGED OUR WORLD

COLA

FINGER PRINT

REGULAR

CEREAL

RIDDLELAND

Designs by Freepik.com

TABLE OF CONTENTS

Chapter Three: Accidental Discovery of Items Outside the House

INTRODUCTION

"There are no rules. That is how art is born,
how breakthroughs happen. Go against the rules or
ignore the rules. That is what invention is about."
▮▮▮▮▮   ~ Helen Frankenthaler   ▮▮▮▮▮

When most people think of discoverers, they think of explorers such as Juan Ponce de Leon. If you recall, the Spanish explorer Ponce de Leon was trying to find the Fountain of Youth. He believed that it was in Florida, and therefore he led the first Western European expedition into Florida. He failed in his quest to find the Fountain of Youth, but he succeeded in discovering an unknown land and history changed because of his discovery.

Many inventors have followed a similar path. The typical inventor begins with a quest, such as finding a cure for cancer, making a lighter tire, or making a brighter light for a surgery room. As they mix chemicals and build devices to try to find the perfect combination to resolve the problem, they create numerous mixtures and find numerous chemical mixtures that do not work. However, sometimes the inventor realizes that, even though the mixture does not solve the problem the inventor was trying to solve, it does solve a problem people have. This accidental discovery is then marketed, and the new invention becomes a part of daily life.

Numerous inventions have been created through accidental discoveries. In all cases, the inventor did not seek to discover them, but upon coming across them, the inventor realized that what had been discovered could solve a problem people had in daily life. Many of these inventions have gone on to become common, everyday items that we still use today. The accidental discovery of the common everyday items mentioned in this book - from bulletproof vests to snow globes, from the color mauve to Scotchgard - changed the world forever.

This book is not just a book of the history of everyday objects; this book is an inspiration. The stories remind us that all people fail, even great thinkers. Inventors seldom get it right the first time, and most typically have to try numerous times. Just like them, you and I will experience times of frustration as we try to reach our goals, and, just like them, we shouldn't let setbacks stop us.

The stories also remind us to keep an open mind. In life, you will encounter brick walls that are too hard to move and impossible to climb over. When you find one of these walls in your path, remember what the inventors did – they went a different direction. You have probably heard the saying that "when life gives you lemons, make lemonade". As you are going to read, when it became obvious that a glass ball filled with water and glitter in it couldn't be used for a surgical light, the inventor decided to stop worrying about making surgical lights and wondered what he could do with the glass ball full of water and glitter– and that is how we got the snow globe.

This book is written with the busy person in mind. Each story takes approximately ten minutes and can be read during brief downtimes. The stories are both entertaining and informative, and they can be read in any order. The book provides insight into how the everyday world around us came to be and is also a testimony to the perseverance and ingenuity of the human spirit.

I find these stories both informative and truly inspirational. I hope you will too.

Riddleland Bonus

Join our Facebook Group at
Riddleland For Kids to get daily jokes and riddles.

Bonus Book

https://pixelfy.me/riddlelandbonus

Thank you for buying this book. As a token of our appreciation, we would like to offer a special bonus—a collection of 50 original jokes, riddles, and funny stories.

CHAPTER ONE:

ACCIDENTAL DISCOVERY OF YUMMY FOODS

"Food is everything we are. It's an extension of nationalist feeling,
ethnic feeling, your personal history,
your province, your region, your tribe, your grandma.
It's inseparable from those from the get-go."
— Anthony Bourdain

1: A Deposed Dictator's Dashed Dream - Power, Money, and Chicle

Do you recognize the name Antonio Lopez de Santa Anna? He was the Mexican President who launched the attack on the Alamo in San Antonio, Texas, in 1836. (You do remember the Alamo, don't you?) Did you know that Santa Anna played a major part in creating an accidental discovery as well?

It was approximately twenty years after that historic battle that Santa Anna found himself in New York talking to Thomas Adams, an inventor. Although Santa Anna had served several terms as Mexican President, his party was no longer in power, and he found himself in exile. Santa Anna believed he could become President of Mexico again, but to do so would take money. Santa Anna was in New York to pitch an idea for an invention with Thomas Adams that he hoped would earn him all the money he needed.

Santa Anna believed that it was somehow possible to turn a chicle - a tarlike, milky, latex product found in Mexico and Central America - into rubber, and he thought Adams was the person who could find the way. Santa Anna had connections in Mexico and could get chicle cheaply; he even brought some to New York for Adams to experiment on. Adams realized that a substitute for rubber would indeed sell well, and so he tried to invent the fake rubber to make them both rich. After a year with no success, he gave up and Santa Anna let the project drop.

Although Santa Anna and the concept of chicle being turned into rubber were out of Adams's life, all the chicle still remained. What was Adams to do with it? He thought and thought, and then he had a moment of inspiration when he saw a girl walk into a drug store and get some paraffin wax chewing gum. He recalled how Santa Anna had said natives sometimes chewed chicle, so Adams decided to ask the pharmacist to sell samples of the chicle as chewing gum. He got reports that the customers said it was good, but Adams realized their reaction could be better. Adams added drops of flavoring into the chicle. Customers at the drugstore loved it! His son, a salesperson, agreed to try to sell the product where he traveled; soon the orders were piling in. Adams eventually invented a machine that made round pellets of the flavored chicle; we call those round pellets . . . **chewing gumballs.**

Have you ever dropped something? People drop things all the time. Some things fall into the sink. Some fall into the toilet. Some hit the floor. Occasionally, we can catch the dropped object before it lands. Dropping things is something everybody does.

Monica Flin dropped something, and it changed Mexican food forever. Monica was a restaurant employee at El Charro restaurant in Tucson, Arizona in the 1920s. Monica was making food in the back kitchen when she dropped the burrito that she had made seconds earlier. (If you have ever been in a restaurant kitchen, you know that fryers are right beside workstations, so that the cook can remove the item from the fryer and then quickly prepare it.) As you would expect, the burrito Monia dropped fell into the cooking oil in the fry vat, hitting the cooking oil hard, creating a splash. The splash threw boiling oil onto Monica's arm, and, without thinking, she began to curse loudly.

Suddenly aware that her relatives were in the back, that her coworkers were staring at her, and that the customers could hear her, she changed her cuss word of "chingoa" to a nonsense word. She smiled guiltily and then got the dip-net to retrieve the dropped burrito from the vat. She fished the burrito out of the fryer and set it on a prep tray. Curious about how a fried burrito would taste; she ate a bite - it tasted wonderful.

Today fried burritos are often served with sour cream, guacamole sauce, and peppers. They come in beef, pork, and chicken. We don't call them fried burritos, however. We refer to them by the nonsense word that Monica called that first one . . . **chimichanga**.

Do you like to impress people? I know that I do. When someone important is going to be watching me, I get nervous. Although people tell me to remember that this is just another person, if it is someone I respect, I find not being nervous hard to do.

Henri Charpentier found it hard to do too. Henri was a 14-year-old working as an assistant waiter at a Paris café in 1895 when, of all people, the Prince of Wales, the future king of the United Kingdom, and his friends, both male and female, sat down at his table as his guest. Henri greeted them, took their orders, and then went to the back to prepare their food for them.

You have probably seen how restaurants have a small flame burning under dishes in buffet lines to keep the food warm; well, Henri was using such a dish to keep pancakes and sauce warm in the back kitchen while he prepared more food. Suddenly, the flame from the candle leapt up and the food caught fire. Henri quickly put the fire out, but feared the food was ruined.

He tasted the food before throwing it out to see if it was salvageable; he really didn't have the time to start over. What he tasted was delicious – it was fit for a king; in this case, fit for a prince. Henri brought the food to the prince and waited nervously. As the prince's friends watched, the prince cut into the pancakes and took a bite. He smiled in wonder, and those around him began to eat as well. The prince loved the result, and even though he had used a fork to eat the pancakes, he used a spoon to gather every drop of syrup.

The prince was so impressed with the dish that he asked Henri what it was called. Thinking fast, Henri decided to dedicate it to the prince. He said, "Crepes Princesse."

To some people, that may have sounded like an insult. Did he just call the prince a "princess"? Luckily, the prince was not insulted – but he was not happy with the name. The prince realized that French, like a lot of languages, has gender pronouns for objects, and pancakes happened to be female. Knowing that Henri's name for the product did not translate well into English, the prince pointed to the lady across the table from him and said to give it her first name. Today, what was originally called "Crepes Princesse" we call . . . **Crepes Suzette.**

Are you one of those people who is never satisfied with the status quo? Are you someone who likes to try new things? Do you ever wonder "what if?" For instance, the other night we were having ice cream and I wondered to myself what would it taste like if I added peanut-butter? What if I added ketchup? What if I added peanut butter and ketchup? I kind of grossed out my family, but I thought they were good questions.

Curt Jones had that kind of inquiring mind. In 1987, Curt Jones was working in a chemical lab flash-freezing animal food. (Flash freezing is where the food is frozen so quickly that it does not have time to develop ice crystals.) As he worked, he asked himself, "What if I flash freeze homemade ice cream instead of churn it?" Curt was not only a thinker; he was a doer – so he decided to try to flash freeze drips of ice-cream.

Most ice cream contains air, but when that same base was dropped into liquid nitrogen, Curt found that it froze immediately, without air and without ice crystals, forming dots of ice-cream. By adding different flavorings into the ice-cream base, he was able to create different flavors of dots; the first flavors included strawberry, chocolate, vanilla, strawberry cheesecake, Neapolitan, and peanut-butter.

Dots of ice cream, what a joke, he thought. He personally liked the taste though, so he sought the opinion of his friends and neighbors. The item was greeted warmly, so he opened a store to sell it in Lexington, Kentucky; the store closed nine months later due to a lack of business.

Curt still saw potential in the dots, so he tried selling them at Opryland, a Nashville amusement park. The dots, which he described as the "ice cream of the future" were a popular novelty, and, before long, Walt Disney World in Orlando, Florida, agreed to sell them as well. Although grocery stores cannot sell his product because it melts so quickly, you can find his product at a lot of amusement parks and shopping malls where it is packed in dry ice until it is ready to be distributed. When you go to these places, you can ask for "ice-cream of the future" or "those ice cream pebbles you dip your spoon in" and the vendor will know what you mean, but most people call this product . . . **Dippin' Dots.**

Don't you get frustrated when your mom nags you about being careful? Whenever we have barbecued chicken my mom suggests I wear a bib-like napkin so that I don't drip anything onto my nice shirt. I typically tell her I have it all under control but, last night I should have listened to her - upon leaving the table, I saw a drop or two of greasy sauce that I didn't realize spilled. Moms know what they are talking about.

Adults are the same way. They think they can be careful and that they are being careful - but sometimes they too find that they were not as careful as they thought they were being. Consider James Schlatter, a chemist who was working to find a cure for ulcers. James was pouring chemicals from flask to flask, and, unknown to him, one of the chemicals splashed onto his finger. He continued his work and later, possibly to turn a page in a book, he licked his finger. His mouth filled with a sugary taste. (Thank goodness he was not working with poison that day; I am sure he got in a lot of trouble for not wearing gloves and washing his hands.)

As he licked his finger, he realized how careless he had been. However, he was all smiles, for he realized he had just discovered a compound that was 200 times sweeter than sugar. He had been working with aspartic acid, and so he named the product aspartame. Marketers, of course, wanted to name it something everyone could pronounce, so today you will see aspartame in most restaurants, often in a blue package, labeled . . . **Equal and Nutra-Sweet.**

6: Cool Kids Have Cool Ideas

    Do you have an opinion about something? I have opinions. For instance, I may think that the White House should be painted green to support the Environmental Movement. I can share my opinion, and, although my friends and family will know of it, likely not much will come of it. On the other hand, if the President of the United States concludes that the White House should be painted green – either through his own thought process or having heard someone share the opinion, then people across the nation hear about the opinion and something is likely to be done. Fair or not, the President is likely to get the credit for the idea. In life, the cool kids often get the credit for something other people have done.

That is not a new principle. In 1904, the coolest place to be in the world was St. Louis, Missouri, at the World's Fair. This was in the days before television and the Internet, so cultures were not as well connected as they are today. The World's Fair was the place to see the latest in technology, to learn about other countries as well as to brag about one's own, and to try novel foods not available elsewhere. If something happened at the World's Fair, it became world-wide news. Everybody who was anybody tried to attend the fair; it was the place where all the cool kids gathered.

Richard Blechynden was, in this sense, one of those cool kids. Richard had the dual title of the India Tea Commissioner and Director of the East Indian Pavilion. In his exhibit, he was offering samples of free hot tea for everyone. Blechynden's goal was to get people interested in his product, and he believed if they would try a cup of hot tea for free, they would likely purchase the product in the future and then tell their friends about it as well.

Things were not going well for Richard this day, though. Missouri is extremely hot and muggy in the summer, so few people were taking him up on his offer of free hot tea. If no one took his tea, the future sales for his company looked bleak. He had to do something.

Richard realized that people needed a cold drink to help them to cool down and to replace the fluids they were losing from sweat. Richard instructed his co-workers to take the brewed tea, fill several large bottles, add ice, and place the bottles on stands upside down so that the tea would flow through iced lead pipes. Richard's invention was a success; the fair goers were very receptive to a free, cold drink of brewed tea.

Historians point out that Richard wasn't the first to come up with cold tea, but he may have thought he was – or he may have seen it or read about it elsewhere. What is for sure is that Richard's booth introduced the beverage to the world. That beverage is still a summertime favorite, and, in many parts of the world, is served year-round. You may never have heard of cold tea; you have likely heard it called . . . **iced tea.**

7: The Magic Root

Have you ever heard the expressions "you are what you eat" and "garbage in, garbage out"? Those expressions remind us that if we make good choices with our foods, we are likely to be healthy and that the reverse is also true - if we eat junk foods our bodies will not be in good shape. Science has supported those statements.

Early civilizations may not have had these exact quotes, but they understood the truth behind them. For instance, they realized that if they ate certain roots, they would be healthy, and they knew if they chose to eat certain other roots, they would become ill. Ancient people did not understand how things worked, but they did recognize cause-and-effect relationships.

One of the plants the ancients believed was good for the body was a licorice plant, an herbaceous shrub. They believed that the plant's root helped do away with allergies, get rid of sore throats, and reduce swelling of inflammations. Archeologists have proof that all major cultures – Chinese, Greek, Roman, and Egyptian used it for all these purposes. These cultures may have perceived it more as magic than we do, but they knew there were helpful chemicals in it. The root wasn't just something for the superstitious peasants; the root was revered by royalty too, and it has even been found in a Pharaoh's tomb.

Some people just don't care for medicine, so they would place the root in their water and other beverages. This caused the drink to take on the flavor of the root. Whereas these people may not have liked the taste of the root, the majority of people loved the taste, and so they too began to add the root into their drinks. Soon, people began to wonder if they could munch on the root as a snack instead of diluting it. The answer was yes.

The root became a sweet treat for children of Northern Europe. Knowing that it was medicine and that it had some vitamin-like qualities in it, parents often gave the root guilt-free to their children. They thought they were doing their children a favor. (They didn't realize how much sugar it had or how the sugar could make children hyper.)

Today's scientists aren't as convinced about the root's medicinal purpose as ancient people were, but you can still find the root in some brands of cough drops. Today, the root is considered primarily a candy. You have probably had some of this magic root. . . **licorice.**

Barney and Allen Hartman loved moonshine (illegal, home-made whiskey). They liked their moonshine mixed with a lemon lime drink, but the mixture they craved was not available in the part of Tennessee where they had just moved from Georgia in the late 1930s. Rather than drive back to Georgia or pay to have the mixture shipped, they developed their own. They called the mixture Mountain Dew. They liked their alcohol in it, but they also liked the mixture as a beverage by itself - and they thought others would too. However, other people did not prefer their recipe. Whereas other lemon-lime sodas were competing well with colas in the market, people kept choosing Sprite and 7-Up over their Mountain Dew, and in frustration the brothers sold the recipe for $6.95 in the 1950s to Tip Corporation.

Tip added lemonade to the Hartman brother's recipe, and the product began to sell well. Pepsi saw what Tip was doing and it recognized the soda's potential. Pepsi bought the product in 1964. In 1974, it added orange flavoring to the recipe and a green dye. When it made these changes, Pepsi kept the name Mountain Dew, but it did away with the hillbilly motif.

Pepsi has continued to innovate the product. It has created new flavors, including cherry, which Pepsi named Code Red. Pepsi has tried to place the product in niches such as extreme sports and computer gaming. It has even tested specific flavors in specific restaurants, such as Baja Blast at Taco Bell restaurants.

Like many products, as the product evolved the product changed its name. Today, you don't see the name "Mountain Dew" on anything. In the 1990s when Pepsi was placing Mountain Dew into extreme sports, it took extreme steps and removed the vowels in "Mountain"; today, you know the product as . . . **Mtn Dew.**

Have you ever tried to do something nice for a friend, and then other people want in on the act too? I used to write stories about my friends in school for them to read; the other kids saw me doing this, and they asked that they be put in the story too. Sometimes when you do something nice for one-person, other people also hope to get that same act of kindness.

This happened to Margaret Rudkin. Margaret was the mother of three children, one of which had asthma and food allergies. The doctors had concluded that preservatives in food upset her child's body, so she baked him a special wheat bread.

The bread without the chemical preservatives in it made a big difference to her son's health. When she went to the doctor next time, the doctor asked how the boy was doing. She explained that he was doing much better, and she explained that she was making a special wheat bread for him.

The doctor had other patients who were suffering with similar allergies and asthma. The doctor told them about what Margaret had said, and, wanting the best for their children, the parents of these children approached Margaret about baking some of her wheat bread for their children too. Margaret agreed to do it. Meanwhile, Margaret's husband worked on Wall Street, and he had talked about the product to people - and they wanted to buy some too. Margaret agreed to bake bread for them too. Margaret used a lot of natural ingredients in her bread, and she passed the cost on to her customers – her homemade bread was double the store-bought brand – but her customers didn't care. The more she baked, the more her reputation grew, and the more demand there was for her bread. Margaret had not set out to create a new food; she had simply been trying to help her son, but there was no doubt she had invented a unique bread.

Margaret lived in Fairfield, Connecticut on a 123-acre farm. The farm was dotted with pepperidge trees, and so she and her husband called the farm Pepperidge Farm. When Margaret started to bake bread for other people, they referred to it by where she lived; they referred to it as . . . **Pepperidge Farm bread.**

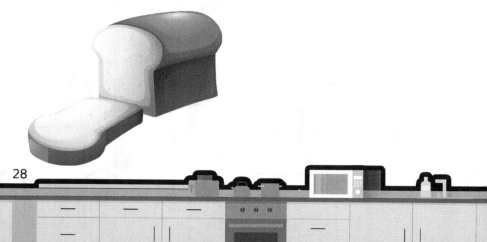

Pharmacists used to mix more than just medicines in their drug stores. Many had soda fountains, where they served drinks they created. In most cases, these drinks were not only marketed for taste but also because of their healing qualities.

Caleb Bradham owned such a pharmacy in New Bern, NC. In 1893, he put together a mixture of sugar, water, caramel, lemon oil, kola nuts, nutmeg and other additives which was supposed to aid in digestion. He called the mixture "Brad's Drink," referring to his last name. Whether it was the taste or the fact that the mixture really did aid digestion, the drink was so popular, that he began selling the syrup to other pharmacies throughout North Carolina.

He changed the name in 1903 to what it is today, and by 1910 he had franchisers in 24 states. Although it was originally marketed as a digestive aid with the slogan, "Exhilarating, Invigorating, Aids Digestion," by 1910 Bradham realized that people bought the soft drink for the taste and not the medical properties, so Bradham hired a celebrity spokesperson, popular race-car driver Barry Oldfield, to pitch the beverage as the drink that "satisfies."

You have likely tasted Brad's Drink. It is available in lots of restaurants and in most supermarkets. Parents still give this soft drink to their kids – at least mine do – for an upset stomach, although it no longer makes those advertising claims. It was the first soft drink to be allowed into Russia when the Cold War ended. Caleb decided "Brad's Drink" didn't have the marketing flare needed to succeed, so he changed the name in 1903 to what you know it by today . . . **Pepsi.**

Have you ever been to the circus? The circus has some of the most unique sights you will ever see. For instance, you may see lions jump through hoops, witness dogs dance, and watch elephants bat a ball back and forth to each other; you will see people who can walk across a tightrope, acrobats who swing in the air, and motorcycle stuntmen climb walls on their motorcycles. In addition to the main attraction, circuses often offer sideshows of things not normally seen, such as an extremely tall person, a man with excessive tattoos, and a rare animal. Even the food at circuses is rare and different.

In 1857 people didn't have refrigerators, so iced drinks on hot days were rare. The circus was one place that iced drinks were

available. On hot summer days, lemonade was a fast seller. Lemonade - a beverage consisting of lemon juice, water, and sugar - had been in the United States since the 1600s when European immigrants brought it with them from Europe. Ice with lemonade, though, was a real treat.

One summer day in 1857, Pete Conklin was running the circus lemonade stand. Lemonade was selling fast, and a new batch needed to be made. Pete told the next customer standing in front of him that he would be right back and then went out of sight to make a new batch. He grabbed a tub of water and started to add the sugar and the lemons. He then took a large spoon and began to stir the mixture. Imagine his surprise when he started to stir the mixture and noticed a pair of pink tights that had been placed in the water to soak. Imagine his horror when he realized his stirring had caused the dye from the tights to release into the water.

The customers were calling for him to hurry up; he didn't have time to start over. A firm believer in "the show must go on," he brought the pink mixture to his customers. With showman flair, he introduced it as strawberry lemonade - referring to the color and not the fact that it had strawberries in it, but he wasn't going to correct people if they thought it had strawberries in it. People loved the drink! In fact, Conklin's sales doubled. Strawberry lemonade was not available at the grocery stores, and the only place to get it was the circus. Soon, strawberry lemonade was available at all circuses.

Although the red coloring in pink lemonade may come from strawberries, raspberries, or cranberries, even today the red coloring in the lemonade is often a dye. The government has created truth-in-advertising laws and misleading ads are discouraged; therefore, the product Conklin called strawberry lemonade goes by a different name today; we call it . . . **pink lemonade.**

Do you like flowers? Most people do. Flowers are even given as gifts on Mother's Day, Valentine's Day, and special occasions. Most people use flowers as decorations. However, did you know that many flowers have chemicals in them that can be used in medicines?

Michael Sueda was enjoying a cigar while studying feverfew, a daisy-like plant known to relieve headaches, at the University of Illinois in 1937. (Back in the 1930s, people did not know about the health dangers of smoking or think about how the smoke could affect things in the lab.) He set his cigar by the feverfew and walked across the room to get supplies. When he came back and took a drag on his cigar, he noticed a sweet taste that was not there before.

He concluded that the flowers had interacted with his cigar, and he had just discovered a taste that no one had ever experienced - the taste of sodium cyclamate, a substance 30-50 times sweeter than natural sugar. (This may sound like a lot, but, of all the artificial sweeteners, it is the lowest.) He also discovered that, whereas natural sugar stays with the body, this artificial sugar did not, making it perfect for those who wanted to enjoy the taste of sugar without the calories and weight gain that normally resulted from sugar.

Sodium cyclamate is generally known as "cyclamate", and it has been found to be bad for the body in some cases. Because the sweetness is not as strong as most artificial sugars, it is usually mixed with another fake sugar. The other fake sugar is 300-400 times sweeter than sugar but leaves a bitter aftertaste on its own. When mixed 10 parts cyclamate with one part of the other sugar, both sugars taste great. The resulting fake sugar is marketed under the other fake sugar's name . . . **Saccharin.**

Have you ever gotten so involved in something that you don't want to quit? I have said to my mom many times when she called my sister and me to come inside the house from playing outside, "Can I have just a minute or two more, mom?" and I have heard my friends say to their mothers, "I'll be there in a minute, mom." When things are rolling along well, most people don't like to quit.

John Montagu, the Fourth Earl of Sandwich, shared this personality. John enjoyed playing cards, and when he started playing, he didn't like to quit. That didn't mean, though, that John didn't get hungry, so one day in 1762 while playing cards he called for the house cook to bring some food to him. He didn't want to have to get up, he didn't want to have to use a knife and fork, he didn't want to get his fingers dirty – all of that would have interfered with his card game, but he still wanted food.

History doesn't say if it was John or the nameless cook who came up with the idea, but it is likely the cook was overwhelmed. John thought about what he had said - he didn't want to get his fingers dirty, he didn't want to use a knife and fork, and yet he wanted to eat - and he began to think how he could do all of that. John had been to Greece and Turkey and had seen how people there sometimes dipped bread in sauce and added another piece of bread onto it, so, when the overwhelmed cook just stood there in a stunned silence, John likely told the cook to use a slice of bread like a plate, add cheese, meat, sauces and other ingredients, and then use another slice of bread so that no food item except the bread had to be touched.

The house cook then went to the kitchen and followed the recipe. He put two pieces of bread with sauces and other ingredients in the middle and brought it to John at the card table. John's friends had never seen anything like it, and they were amazed at both the eye-appeal and the convenience of this new creation. John liked the creation so much that he asked for it again and again, and soon those around him were asking for it too. Rather than try to describe the creation by its ingredients, they sought to come up with a name for it. Out of respect for John's title, the Fourth Earl of Sandwich, they called the creation the name it still has today . . . **the Sandwich.**

14: The Presentation Was Poor but the Food Itself Was Excellent

Have you ever participated in a fad? A fad is something that everybody – or so it seems – is doing at the moment. Some fads that you or your parents may remember seeing or even being a part of are wearing jeggings, clicking clackers, spinning fidget spinners, catching Pokemon, wearing bell-bottom jeans, doing "the wave" at the stadium, wearing plaid pants, and playing Uno. Fads come and go.

One of the fads in the early 1900s was loose-meat sandwiches. Hamburger was ground, cooked, and mixed into a sauce before being put into a hamburger roll. The dish went by a lot of names, and no two tasted exactly the same – the Barbeque, Beef Mironton, Chopped Meat Sandwiches, Hamburg a la

Creole, Minced Beef Spanish Style, Spanish Hamburgers, the Tavern Burger, and Toasted Deviled Hamburgers, to name a few.

Joe worked at the Maid-Rite Sandwich Shop in Sioux City, Iowa. (Maid-Rite was a chain of sandwich shops and is still in operation today.) Like almost all cafes and sandwich shops at the time, Maid-Rite offered a loose-meat sandwich. When Joe made a loose meat sandwich, he liked to put his ground beef into tomato sauce. Now, even though the hamburger was in small chunks, most restaurants placed the meat on the bun neatly — but that's not how it was done at this Maid-Rite sandwich shop. Joe put on a scoop of meat and let it fall out of the bun. He made great food, but he was sloppy. Joe hadn't meant for the meat to fall out; he was just sloppy.

The patrons noticed this. In the 1930s, "Sloppy Joe" was an insulting term for any café or sandwich shop that made fast food. (When we want to insult those kinds of places today, we call those places "greasy spoons." Somebody likely punned, "You're kind of sloppy there, Joe," and someone else joined in, "Give me one of those Sloppy Joe sandwiches."

Joe's recipe gradually bumped other loose meat sandwiches off the menu at other restaurants, and all loose meat sandwiches began to be known as the Sloppy Joe. In the 1960s Manwich introduced Sloppy Joe meat in a can, bringing the Sloppy Joe fad to the home as well as the restaurant. Some people like to add peppers and onions to the hamburger; others like ketchup, mustard, and/or pickle. No matter which condiments are added, ground hamburger in tomato sauce on a bun is still always referred to as . . . **Sloppy Joe.**

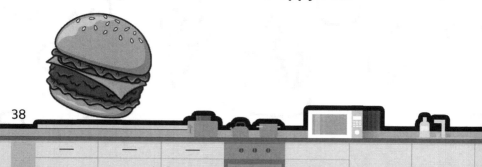

People tend to take things for granted – until something goes wrong. For instance, most of us don't think about how lucky we are to be healthy – until we get sick; we don't think about breathing until we can't catch our breath. Likewise, we don't think about how important our refrigerator is – we take it for granted – until it breaks down, and then getting it fixed is all we can think about.

Omar Knedlik owned a Dairy Queen in Coffeeville, Kansas in 1958. One hot summer day, the refrigerator's cooling mechanism broke. Knedlik immediately called someone to fix it but was told it would be a while before someone could get out to fix it. In the meantime, he had to keep his sodas and other products cold, so he put them in the freezer. As the name suggests, the freezer not only keeps things cool, but it also freezes them. Before Knedlik was conscious of what was happening, the contents inside his Coca-Cola bottles began to freeze.

When customers asked for a bottle of Coca-Cola, Knedlik went to the freezer to get a bottle. He was shocked that the contents had already started to freeze. He had no other Coca-Cola in the store, though, so he took a bottle up front to offer his customer. To his surprise, the customer agreed to accept the bottle, tried it, and loved it. Other customers wanted to try the flavored ice too, and Knedlik readily sold the slushie drink.

Knedlik's slushy drink was so popular that he created a machine that could make the drink. Today, we call that slushie drink the ICEE, and it can be found in many gas stations in a variety of flavors. The story doesn't stop there, though. The Seven-Eleven convenience store chain licensed the technology of the machine from Knedlik in 1965. They added their syrup to create a competing slushy beverage. That beverage surpassed the ICEE in popularity and in pop culture references; it was named for the loud slurping sound people make when drinking it; we call it . . . **the Slurpee.**

Have you ever misheard something that somebody says to you? For instance, you may have thought they greeted you by saying, "Go away" but they really said, "Good day." This miscommunication can make you mad, get you in trouble, or, if you get lucky, can lead to the discovery of something new.

Two college students at Queen Elizabeth College in London, England were working in the chemistry lab in 1976. One student called across the room to his partner to test a chlorine compound. The other student, though, heard his friend, but he heard the word "taste" instead of "test," so guess what happened – that student tasted the chlorine compound. (Never, ever taste things in science class unless the teacher tells you it is okay, and, if you have any doubts, ask again to make sure you heard the teacher correctly.) Luckily, the student was okay.

Because the product combined sucrose and chloride - in scientific terms, it took three hydrogen-oxygen atoms from the sugar and replaced them with chlorine atoms - to form an artificial sweetener 600 times sweeter than sugar, the researchers named it sucralose, reflecting "sugar" and "losing." Unlike other sugar substitutes such as Equal and Saccharin invented before it, this one attached itself to the body, but not nearly to the degree normal sugar does. You might think that sticking partially to the body would mean that no one would be interested in it; but that was not the case. Unlike the others, this sugar substitute could be used for baking, and therefore. it had a lot of possibilities. You have probably seen sucralose; it comes in a yellow wrapper. The marketers didn't think the name "sucralose" would sell a lot of units, so they changed the name to one that would. . . **Splenda.**

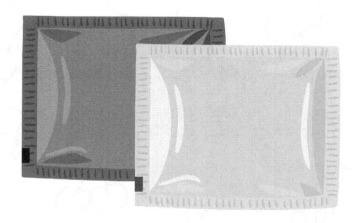

How many times per day do you wash your hands? You should wash them after each trip to the restroom, before meals, before bed, and any time that you are going to put something in your mouth. My guess is that your mom has gotten onto you about handwashing. Mine often says I don't keep them under the water long enough; I'm sure your mom has made a comment or two as well. (Parents care.) Believe it or not, though, sometimes even adults forget to wash their hands.

Constantin Fahlberg was a chemist at John Hopkins University in 1897. Like all people do, he got hungry; he got so hungry, in fact, that he began to eat his lunch without washing his hands. As a chemist, this can literally be a deadly mistake. Fortunately, on this day he had been working with coal tar, and it was not poisonous. His lunch was finger-licking good, and, as he licked his fingers, he tasted something sweet like sugar.

He didn't know what that sweetness was, but he realized that it had to come from the materials he was working with. He continued to do research on the substance and realized that it literally passed through the body; this meant that someone could enjoy great taste without the calories (weight gain) that comes with normal sugar. He named his product "saccharin", which is the Latin word for "sugar". You may not recognize the name "saccharin", but you have probably seen this artificial sweetener in pink packets, especially in caddies sitting by the sugar at restaurants; the product has the brand name . . . **Sweet and Low.**

Have you ever tried to cover up a mistake? I've done it many times. For instance, I was trying to draw a picture of a man walking, but the man looked like a flower instead, so I told everyone I was drawing a picture of a flower. It is okay to admit it; we have all made an embarrassing mistake and then tried to cover it up, hoping no one would ever realize it was a mistake.

Stephanie Tatin made a mistake one day. She and her sister ran a bed and breakfast, the Hotel Tatin, in Paris in the 1880s. Stephanie did most of the cooking, and one night in 1888 she was supposed to make an apple pie. She had put the apples on to cook in butter and cinnamon, but then forgot about them. That proved to be a big mistake, for they started to burn. Smelling that something was wrong, Stephanie suddenly remembered the apples and rushed to turn off the stove.

It appeared too late. The apples were burnt; anyone could see that. Stephanie was short on time, though; she didn't have time to recook the apples. She needed to find a way to cover up her mistake; to make people think that she deliberately burned the apples. Hoping the apples still tasted good – they certainly didn't look very good. She took a spoon and tasted the apples; they tasted very good; in fact, she had accidentally created a caramel sauce that was absolutely delicious. The apples were servable if she could just hide them. Then she had an idea. Normally pie crust goes on the bottom, but who was to say it had to do that? To cover up her mistake, Stephanie put the pie crust on top. She and her sister then served the food to their guests.

Their guests noticed the burnt apples – but in a good way. They couldn't see them, but they sure could taste them – and they loved the taste. The dish was so popular that the guests asked that it be made again. Soon, it became the signature dish of their inn. Guests began to call the dish the tart of Tatin because it was the dessert of the Tatin sisters. Today, we don't call it tart of Tatin, we call it . . . **Tarte Tatin.**

Christmas, birthdays, and other gift-giving occasions are always fun around my house. I like to be surprised and receive new things. Sometimes, though, it is the box, not the gift that gets the most attention. I remember one Christmas when my dad got my mom a large garbage can for Christmas. (It wasn't the most romantic of gifts, but perhaps he had something hidden in it. I just remember the garbage can.) My sister and I played in the box for hours.

Thomas Sullivan encountered a similar problem of people liking the container instead of just the product as he had intended. Thomas was a tea importer in 1908, and he shipped tea across the United States. In the early 1900s, tea was typically shipped in tin canisters. These tin canisters were expensive so, to increase his profits, Thomas wanted to find another way to ship tea. He decided to send the tea in silk bags. Knowing that the change from a tin canister to a silk bag might not be popular, Thomas put just enough tea leaves in each silk bag for a specific serving. Not only did this save him money, but it also reduced tea waste by his customers. Even though he was using silk bags to help his profit margin, he could promote it as if he were trying to help the consumer.

Thomas envisioned that his customers would tear open the silk bag and pour the contents into the tea maker; Thomas designed the silk bag to be a wrapper, not part of the product. To his surprise though, the people who bought the tea in the individual bags began to contact him, asking him for more. In their letter, they explained that, thanks to his bag, they did not need a tea maker any longer. All they had to do was add hot water and let the tea steep.

Over time, small changes were to be made. The tea leaves needed to be able to move and water needed to be able to get to them and yet the tea leaves could not be too free or break apart; Thomas found gauze worked a lot better than silk in meeting this requirement. Although Thomas's clients had figured out how to brew tea using hot water and the silk bags Thomas had provided; Thomas himself was the first to provide step-by-step directions on how to use the bag without a tea maker. When he wrote the directions, he called the product the name that we know it by today . . . **the tea bag.**

What a difference a choice of words can make. For instance, I can describe my mom as "as beautiful as the first day of spring" or as "she looks like the end of a long, hard winter" – it is the same day, but the second is not appealing to my mom. Similarly, I knew of a government official who was referred to as a "civil servant" by those who liked him and as a "bureaucrat" by those who did not like him; both terms mean "government official," but one term made me respect him and the other made me get frustrated with him.

Lou Oldani made a choice of words that birthed a new taste sensation. Lou Oldani owned Mama Campisi's, an Italian restaurant located in a fashionable part of St. Louis, Missouri. One night, Fritz, a cook, was making scaloppini for a customer. The restaurant used wine for cooking, and, on this evening, the cook had been drinking the wine when no one was looking. Fritz was tipsy from the wine, and he accidentally dropped some ravioli into the fry vat. Lou's wife, Evelyn, saw him pull the ravioli out and sought to salvage them. (In the restaurant business, wasted food is wasted money.)

She let them drip-dry over the vat, set them on a tray, and then sprinkled Parmesan cheese on them. She sent them to the bar as appetizers. It just happened that Mickey Garagiola, the baseball player Joe Garagiola's older brother, was at the bar counter that evening with his friends; Mickey was the first to try one. He had never seen anything like it – and he had never tasted anything like it. Lou's restaurant had hit a home run!

Mickey, of course, wanted to know how they were made, so he turned to Lou. Lou had been in the restaurant business long enough to know that a description can make or break a product, no matter how good it tastes. Lou wanted to create a mouth-watering image for the fried product, so, instead of saying "fat fried," "deep fried", or "greasy fried," he told Mickey the ravioli were "toasted". Today, we know those fried golden pillows of dough filled with meat as . . . **toasted ravioli.**

Do you like to add a little spice to things? Some foods are kind of boring, so you likely jazz them up with salt and pepper, ketchup and mustard, relish and mayonnaise, and whatever other sauces and spices you love. Usually these spices enhance the food, but some spices just do not go well with certain foods. In many cases, the only way to see how a spice will affect a food is to try it.

Trying to enhance basic food with spices and condiments is nothing new. Over 2,000 years ago, a cook in China wanted to flavor some soybeans. He took boiled, ground soybeans and added impure sea salt, thinking he was going to get a salty soybean. The sea salt, though, contained chemicals that caused the soy mixture to curdle. The result definitely did not taste like a salty soybean!

The result was not what the chef anticipated at all, but just because it was not the anticipated result did not mean that it was a bad result. The resulting bean curds were low in calories, high in protein, and a great source of iron. They could be readily added to other dishes, and their flavor varied based on what they were paired with. The recipe for the bean curds quickly spread throughout the Orient, including to Japan, Korea, and Vietnam. When people from these nations migrated to the United States, they brought their love for this food with them.

Today bean curds are still created by turning the soybeans into curds, which are then pressed into a white block. These bean curds have many uses, including serving as a meat substitute. Some people still call the resulting product bean curds, but you likely know this 2000-year-old accidental discovery as . . . **tofu.**

Have you ever stood with a cereal bowl talking to someone, and then someone else walks by you and bumps into you, causing your cereal to slosh out? What a mess!

A doctor at Washburn-Crosby Company in 1921 was apparently doing exactly that in the breakroom, when somebody nudged his elbow, causing him to spill his wheat gruel onto a hot stovetop. To his amazement, the wheat became crispy flakes.

American breakfast used to consist of ham, eggs, and bacon when the majority of people worked on farms in the 1800s, but now the majority of people had become urbanites in the early 1900s, breakfast had changed to cereals such as Grape Nuts, a product Washburn-Crosby sold. Health officials were stating that Americans needed more fiber in their diet, and the doctor was practicing what he preached when he ate his bowl of gruel.

The doctor realized the wheat flake had potential, and he could picture it doused in milk to help people meet their fiber needs. He shared his idea with the factory managers, and they agreed. When they tried to mass produce it, though, the early versions of the cooked wheat broke apart in shipping. In 1922, the head miller, George Cormack, came up with a wheat flake that did not break in shipping. He named the product Washburn's Gold Medal Whole Wheat Flakes. Washburn Crosby Company later changed its name to General Mills, a company you have probably heard of, and the company had a contest to determine what to rename the cereal. Jane Bausman, an employee's wife, came up with the winning name, the name you know of the crispy wheat cereal by today . . . **Wheaties.**

Have you ever put something in storage and then forgotten about it? Many people put things in the attic, others put things in the basement, some put things in the cellar, a few place things in sheds, and others put things in storage units – these stored items are typically forgotten about. Out of sight means out of mind. In time, when we return to the storage facility to hunt for something else, we come across this wonderful treasure we had completely forgotten that we had.

Something similar happened to John Lea and William Perrins, two drug store owners in Worcester, England. They had been asked by Lord Marcus Sandys, a former Governor of Bengal, India, in 1837 to try to create the taste sensation of the fish sauce he had enjoyed so much in India. At Lord Sandys' request, John and William had put together a mixture of fish and vegetables, but it smelled so bad that they placed it in the cellar, so it didn't stink up the whole store. A few days later they gave Lord Sandy a bottle of the fish sauce as promised. Although they gave him his bottle, they had some sauce left over which they intended to use themselves and sell to their friends. They left that extra sauce in the cellar. The two pharmacists didn't go to the cellar often, and the sauce was forgotten. Two years later when they went to clean the cellar, they found the leftover mixture where they left it.

The mixture tasted great; it had fermented. They bottled it and sold it - it sold well. Most people used it as a steak sauce, although John and William also promoted it as a lotion that would make your hair grow beautifully – a claim they later dropped. When John and William acquired a contract with British passenger ships to keep their sauce on tables in the dining room, its fame became world-wide.

The bottle had to be wrapped in paper to protect it from breaking at sea, and the bottle still retains that wrap. Today the sauce is still used on steaks, in alcoholic drinks, oysters, deviled eggs, and Caesar salads. When people referred to the sauce, they mentioned the town that it was created in; we still call it by its original name . . . **Worcestershire Sauce.**

Have you ever thought about what all the possibilities are that are literally in your hand? That hand can do so many good things. For instance, you can help someone off the ground, you can work with tools, and you can shake hands as a gesture of friendship. That same hand, though, can be used as a fist to hurt somebody, opened to slap somebody, and brought down hard on something to chop it. Your hand can be used for good purposes or for bad purposes – it is up to you.

Like the hand, lots of objects and living creatures have potential to be extremely helpful or very harmful, depending on how we use them. A great example of this is bacteria. Bacteria provides some of our great medicines; bacteria can also kill you. Bacteria are so small you cannot see them without a good magnifying glass; in fact, you probably have lots of bacteria on you at this moment (Gross!) Believe it or not, this tiny one-cell organism is responsible for one of the first accidental discoveries in history.

This first accidental discovery in food history occurred in about 9,000 B.C. somewhere in the Middle East, quite possibly Turkey. People had begun to domesticate cows, sheep, and goats. Cows had become a source of labor, milk, and meat. If early people did butcher an animal, they did not let any part of the animal go to waste. Even non-food parts were utilized to the best extent possible; for instance, they used the skin for leather and the intestines and stomach for bottles to keep milk and water.

Somehow bacteria got into somebody's container of milk - the milk may have been left in the sun too long or perhaps the vessel wasn't clean - and this accident caused a great discovery. The person who found the fermented milk likely showed it to his friends and asked them to smell (My friends do that to me with gross stuff.) They all looked at each other until finally somebody decided to taste this thick milk. Our unknown hero likely hesitantly drank a swallow, reported that it tasted a tad sour, licked his lips, and then added that it was delicious.

Today, we still eat this fermented milk; in fact, food workers add the bacteria to the milk deliberately to create this product. Also, we still use a Turkish word to describe this tart, thick milk product . . . **yogurt.**

CHAPTER TWO:

ACCIDENTAL DISCOVERY
OF
ITEMS AROUND THE HOUSE

"Have nothing in your house that you do not know to be useful,
or believe to be beautiful."
~ William Morris

25: The Clumsy Maid

When I think of cleaning something, I think about using soap and water. Some fabrics, though, are ruined by water and others cannot survive the heat of the dryer. Also, water is not good at removing grease and oil. Luckily, there are other solvents out there besides water. Any time that something besides water is used for cleaning is referred to as "dry cleaning."

The process of dry cleaning came about as the result of an accident. Jean Baptiste Jolly of France had eaten a delicious meal but had marred the tablecloth with grease stains. (We've all done that, haven't we?) Jean lived before electricity, so if he wanted to see what he was eating, he had to have either a fire in the fireplace or oil lamps around him. Jean was a rich man who had servants. One of the servants went to strip the messy tablecloth from the table, but she knocked over a kerosene lamp, spilling the fuel onto the tablecloth. Jean sat there patiently, trying to help her gather the tablecloth. As he pulled on the tablecloth, he noticed that the spilt turpentine had evaporated – and so had grease stains!

Jean took the tablecloth upstairs and filled his bathtub with turpentine. He then placed the entire tablecloth in the turpentine. Sure enough, when the turpentine dried, the stains were gone. Jean realized that other people had the same laundry problems he did, so he decided to open a store in Paris that specialized in removing such stains. He called the store "Teinturerier Jolly Belin," but, if you saw it, you would refer to it by its English name, . . . **the dry cleaners.**

26: It's a Colorful World!

A few weeks back, I went to the school nurse. Everyone in our class had to go one by one for a vision test. First, she had me cover one eye and read letters on the wall, then she had me look through a lens and read letters, and finally she took out a book and had me name numbers that were in circles – the numbers were one color, and the circles were another color. We came upon one page that did not have a number – trick question, I thought. The nurse insisted there was a number. I insisted there was not. The nurse realized I was color blind. Although I could tell a lot of colors apart, I cannot tell blacks, blues and purples. (My mom inspects my clothes each day to make sure I don't look too dorky.)

Don McPherson had an invention to his name – laser safety goggles. Don did laser surgery on eyes and wore the glasses during surgery to protect his own eyes. The glasses were extremely comfortable, though, and so he and other surgeons wore them casually as sunglasses as well. In 2005, Don was playing Ultimate Frisbee in Santa Cruz, California when one of his friends, Michael Angler, asked to look at his glasses.

Don gave him the glasses and his friend put them on. As Michael's eyes focused, he let out a gasp. Michael had never seen the color orange before. With the glasses on, Michael could clearly see orange. Both realized then and there that, unintentionally, Don had discovered glasses that helped people overcome color blindness.

Don was fascinated with the find and wanted to learn more about color blindness and how to cure it. He and his partner Andy Schmeder founded EnChroma Labs where they studied the cones of the eyes and experimented with various lenses. They were very successful with helping adults with partial color blindness to see the color(s) they were missing. Today, they have expanded their goals to help partially colorblind children and to create lenses for those people who see only in black-and-white.

Colorblindness is a very common problem and many people – such as me – don't even realize we have it. Can you imagine not being able to tell red from green, and you are pulling up to a stop light? Luckily, once colorblindness is identified, Don's special lenses help correct it. Don called these special lenses . . . **EnChroma.**

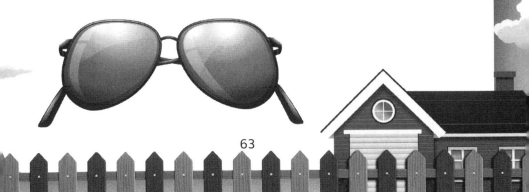

27: Rubbed in the Wrong Way

I like doing chores to help around the house. (All right, I admit, I usually like to do chores to help around the house, but sometimes I do want to go play video games or go outside with my friends instead of finishing my chores.) Many nights after supper, my mom would remove the dishes from the table, I would wash them, and then my sister would dry them. When I washed them, I would always rub them downward real hard, removing all food chunks and hopefully any bacteria that was on them.

John Walker cleaned things the same way. John was a pharmacist, a person who worked at a drug store and mixed chemicals. In 1827 in England, medicine did not always come in the form of a pill; in many cases the pharmacist had to mix the medicine with a mortar and pestle. One day, John was wiping off dried chemicals from a wooden stirring rod he had used to mix medicines when suddenly it sparked and caught fire.

John realized this discovery could be especially useful for starting fires in fireplaces. He experimented with putting a sulfur head on the stick and striking it on a rough surface. Most of the time the product worked, and the flame burned bright, but sometimes the head fell off, and the burning sulfur could catch clothes or carpeting on fire. Word of what John had made spread around town, and people were willing to pay him to make some for them. He hesitantly sold them what they wanted, but he believed the product was flawed so he never patented it.

Because John did not patent it, other people began to experiment with the new concept as well. Isaac Holden started selling his own sulfur-dipped sticks around the world, and, because no one outside of John's little area had ever heard of John, became known as the founder of this discovery . . . **the friction match.**

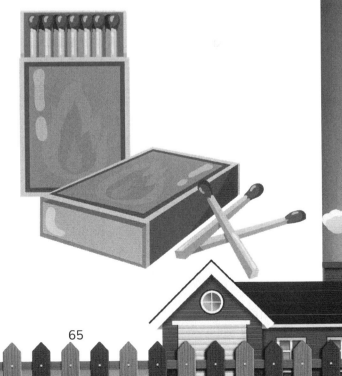

28: One for the Road

Have you ever been in a car trying to drive through the backwoods on a moonless night? It is very, very hard to see. If you haven't done that, perhaps you have played the game "Where's Waldo?" In that game, you are given a picture. Your job is to find Waldo, a boy in a striped shirt; he is somewhere in the picture. Waldo blends into the scenery so well, though, that he is very hard to spot.

Although some of America's backroads still do not have reflective markers, most roads do. When people drive at night, their headlights shine upon those markers, and the paint on them reflects so that the driver can see the marker and keep the car near the marker. Markers are usually located on medians, but sometimes they are on the shoulders of the road too. Believe it or not, these markers were an accidental discovery and they also inspired an accidental discovery.

Bob Switzer was an American who was studying chemistry at the University of California in 1933. In the summer of that year, he got a job unloading tomatoes from railroad freight cars at the H.J. Heinz plant. One day while unloading, he fell and suffered severe injuries. He was told by the doctors to stay in a dark room until he recovered his eyesight, and this took several months.

While in the dark room, Bob thought about how to do magic tricks and experimented with blacklights and fluorescent paints. He continued to experiment once he was allowed out of the darkness, and, in 1934, he invented a neon-colored paint by mixing fluorescent materials with wood varnish. Although Bob was designing it for the toy market, people soon realized he had invented a high-visibility paint that would reflect off headlights and other lighting. He began selling the paint in 1934 through his store, the Flour S. Art Company. Using it for roads was the first use of this accidental discovery.

Bob's business expanded from road medians to other aspects of road safety. States were very concerned about their road workers, and so they began to design construction cones with the paint. Soon they even had workers who wore jackets containing stripes of the reflective paint so drivers could clearly see them.

Bob, too, kept trying to find new uses for the fluorescent paints. He soon realized that the paint could be applied to posters, and he began working with Warner Brothers making

special movie posters. Like other people, Bob also realized the fluorescent paints could be applied to clothes. (One day – don't ask me why – he decided to test his theory that the paint would work on clothes, and he painted with his neon paint on his wife's wedding dress.) Soon rail yard workers, safety inspectors, soldiers, and highway workers were wearing the neon colors. Today, people walking their dogs wear them, children wear them, and even pets wear them. Dance troupes dance in the near-dark, wearing the neon paint so all the audience can see is the painted object. Neon clothing has become both a safety piece and a fashion statement. Bob called the paint on his wife's wedding dress "Day-Glo," but you know the glow-in-the-dark, high-visibility, warning clothing product as . . . **High Viz Clothing**.

29: The Forgetful Chemist

Have you ever forgotten something? My mom took my sister and I yard-sale shopping with her one Saturday morning. When she pulled up for a sale, she let us out of the car so we could look around too. As she shopped, my mom noticed a reseller who was shopping; knowing the reseller was likely to get ahead of her and buy what my mom was searching for, my mom got in the car and left – forgetting all about me and my sister. (Luckily, she remembered us a few minutes later when she noticed we weren't in the car.)

James Gamble, the co-founder's son of Proctor and Gamble Company, was forgetful too. He worked in his parents' business as a chemist. His parents had bought the recipe for Ivorine, an inexpensive white soap, from J.B. Williams in 1840 and now, in 1879, he had been placed in charge of making Ivorine. On this morning James started to make a batch of soap – which he forgot he started; the soap was still churning when James went to lunch. The soap was still churning when James got back for lunch; the soap had churned way too long, allowing way too much air to get into it. The soap was ruined; it could not be salvaged as an Ivorine soap bar.

Not wanting to suffer the financial loss of discarding the product, the company shipped the new soap. It pretended that the accident was intentional, and that James had created just what people needed. The extra air gave the soap a trait other soaps did not have – it floated. Now the soap was not going to get lost or melt unnecessarily in the bathtub.

The floating not only made the soap easy to find in the tub but it also communicated "clean" in people's minds. The soap was well accepted.   Harley Procter, the other founder's son, named the product based on Psalm 45:8, and the product still has the same name today . . . **Ivory Soap.**

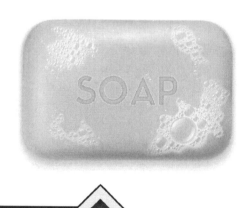

Do you remember when you were about three years old, and you got the opportunity to play with one of those boards that had circles, squares, rectangles, and other shapes drilled in it? Your mission was to find the correct block and stick it/hammer it through the hole - it was a fun way to learn about colors, shapes, and sizes, as well as practice motor skills such as hammering. I know I sometimes got it right; sometimes it took a second or third try. Although I didn't always get it right, I knew that the correct shape was there in the pile of shapes on the floor; I just had to find it.

Thomas Edison used the same strategy. He was in the process of inventing a machine that could both record and reproduce sound, and he knew that he had the right pieces - as well as a lot of wrong pieces. What he did not know was exactly which pieces he needed and in what order to place them. Out of all the many combinations he could have chosen, one day in the summer of 1877 he accidentally guessed right.

On that day, Edison was tinkering with a piece of tinfoil that was used to record telegraph signals and a paper cylinder. As he turned a handle to move the tinfoil, he shouted the nursery rhyme "Mary had a Little Lamb" into the cylinder. Inside the cylinder a needle vibrated from his voice, making a groove into the tinfoil; to his amazement, Edison was able to play it back.

The following spring, Edison recorded crowds and music, amazing people with the sound reproduction. (Unfortunately for us, the recordings could only be replayed five or six times before they were ruined, so they are not available to us.) Seeing the success of his machine, he started producing the machine commercially.

This was Edison's first major discovery; the lightbulb would be his second. He had numerous other inventions as well, but this talking machine was his favorite. Over the years, it has been called the gramophone and the record player, but Edison called it two Greek words, "phone" which means sound and "graph" which means writing; he called it . . . **the Phonograph.**

31: The Nervous Debtor and the Generous Creditor

Have you ever owed somebody money? Being in someone's debt is not a good feeling. Also, if it is not paid back and you signed a contract promising you would pay it back, as an adult, you can get in big trouble.

In 1796, Walter Hunt owed a man $15. (Fifteen dollars is still quite a lot of money when you don't have it, but I checked with the U.S. Department of Labor and, because of inflation, owing $15 in 1796 would be like owing $296 today.) Walter wanted to pay off his debt, but he didn't have that kind of money. As he sat at his desk brainstorming ways to come up with the money, he played with a piece of wire. He coiled the wire into a spring; it had a point at one end and a coil at the other, and the point could slip inside the coil. He placed his finger on the wire as he thought, pushing it in and out of the coil nervously. Suddenly he became conscious of what he was doing – and he realized he had just created a unique pin.

Walter believed that this clasp and spring action had never been thought of, and the U.S. government agreed with him, awarding him a patent for his accidental discovery in 1849. So, what did Walter do with that patent? He sold it to the man he owed $15. It had taken Walter over 50 years to pay his debt, but he paid it. His creditor, an employee of W.R. Grace and Company, saw potential in Robert's invention and did not seek to take advantage of Robert; he gave him $400 for it.

Walter' pin was the first to have a clasp and spring action. Robert claimed that it was intentionally designed this way to keep fingers from injury. His creditor admired that injury-preventing feature and marketed the coiled wire as . . . **the safety pin.**

Have you ever been embarrassed? I know I have been. I asked my dad to video tape me putting the football; he agreed to do it, but, with the camera running, I missed the ball. (My dad still has that clip.) It is embarrassing to fail when you are so confident that you are going to be successful.

In 1923 Richard Drew found himself in an auto body shop. He was an employee of 3M, a company that manufactured sandpaper. Although his passion was to conduct research with cellophane, a recent discovery, the company wanted to use him as an inspector. The company had just come up with a new line,

Wetordry, and Richard was tasked with watching how well it worked for the body shop workers.

The workers used the sandpaper to sand down rust and other spots before putting putty on it and then repainting it. The sandpaper worked great. What didn't work great, Richard noted, was the paper strip that the mechanics used to stop one color from running into another on two-toned cars. He saw that when the mechanics pulled the paper off, the paint came with it.

Richard believed he could help. He created a cellophane tape that was 5 centimeters wide and had glue on both of its edges. The mechanics tried the tape. Unfortunately for Richard, when the wet paint got on the tape, the tape bubbled. One of the mechanics noted that it needed a whole lot more glue and accused Richard of making "Scot's tape." (Scottish people were stereotyped as being frugal, and Richard had been very stingy with the glue.)

Richard went through numerous versions trying to make the perfect tape product. In those trials, he successfully created the first masking tape in history. He went on to perfect the sticky cellophane as well; it was made from adhesive and tree parts called cellulose that had been turned into cellophane. Because the United States was going through the Great Depression in the 1930s and people had to be frugal, being Scottish was something to be proud of. Richard had a product that could mend a tear in paper, take the place of a pin, and so much more. His boss decided to keep the name the mechanic had called it – he named it Scotch Brand Cellulose Tape, but we call it . . . **Scotch Tape.**

Have you ever stepped in doggie doo-doo and gotten it all over your favorite shoes? If you have, you have likely tried to wipe the spot of do-doo with a towel, run water over the offending area, scrub the offending area, and numerous other techniques to get the odor and the residue off the shoe. If you have had such an experience, you can relate to what happened to a research assistant at a 3M lab in 1952.

The lab assistant was assisting Patsy Sherman and Sam Smith, two researchers at 3M, who were trying to create a new rubber to be used for jet fuel lines. Patty had just made a bottle of synthetic latex and handed it to the lab assistant. The lab assistant didn't have a good grip on the glass bottle, though, and accidentally dropped it. The latex splashed on the assistant's white canvas shoes. The assistant could not wash off the latex nor could he or the researchers find a solvent to remove it. The three of them noticed another trait - dirt washed right off the part of the shoes that had been touched by the latex.

Patsy realized that such a chemical could be applied by manufacturers — for instance, car dealers who didn't want prospective customers damaging a test car could coat the car's seats in it — and by parents — for instance, parents who didn't want food stains on their couch could coat the couch in it. 3M began to sell the product in 1956, and a patent was obtained in 1973.

In the 1930s during the Great Depression, 3M had adopted the Scottish motif to suggest being frugal. (People stereotyped people from Scotland as being very frugal, and, in the Great Depression when money was tight, everyone wanted to be frugal.) This product helped ensure one's expensive fabrics lasted longer — hence, one was being frugal even as one shelled out cash for the product — and because it guarded the product and protected it, this new chemical was called . . . **Scotchgard.**

34: Something is in the Air

Have you ever gotten frustrated? How did you deal with that frustration? Do you hit a punching bag? Did you say a bad word? Did you go for a walk? People get frustrated.

Walter Jaeger, a Swiss researcher, was frustrated. Walter was trying to invent a product that would detect poisonous gas. (Carbon-monoxide is a gas that cannot be seen or smelled but can be very deadly. Walter was not the person who discovered this, but, thank goodness, the device was invented. Today, many businesses and homes now have carbon-monoxide detectors.) Walter found ways NOT to invent it, and that helped others find the way to invent it.

Walter had been working on the machine all day - and the machine was not detecting the gas. He was frustrated - and he knew it. Before he did or said something he would regret, he decided to take a break. He could sense he was tense, and he didn't like that feeling.

Walter was a smoker – this was in the late 1930s, years before all the dangers of nicotine were known, so he sat down to relax with a cigarette. He inhaled deeply and then released the smoke and his tensions in the next breath. The smoke drifted across his so-called poison gas detector, making its alarm sound. Shocked and embarrassed, Walter rushed to turn it off.

Walter's invention was not the first invention to detect fire. Fire detecting equipment had been invented by Thomas Edison and Francis Upton in 1890; their device monitored the temperature of the room and sounded the alarm if it got too hot. Walter's device wasn't based on heat, however; Walter's accidental discovery was based on the sensor detecting smoke and air quality changes. Walter's device led to the creation of smoke sensors being placed in industrial buildings a few years later. The cost of these sensors was high though, and the average person could not afford them.

In 1970, people tinkered with the invention, finding ways to reduce costs. Also, as more of the product began to be made, the cost was able to be dropped. People soon realized that the smoke sensor saved lives, and many cities began to create laws that required them to be installed in both public buildings and private homes. This increased the demand even more and made the price drop even further. Today, many homes have a smoke sensor in each room. We don't call these smoke sensors, though; we call them . . . **smoke detectors.**

Ever look at something; think to yourself, "that's not what I need;" and keep on looking for something else. That's exactly what Dr. Harry Coover did – and what he had in his hands was one of the greatest inventions in recent history.

Harry was a scientist working for the United States government in 1942. He wanted to create a strong, clear plastic that could be used to enhance the scope on a rifle. As he messed with various combinations of chemicals, he created cyanoacrylate, a very sticky substance. Because it was so sticky, Harry set it into the discard group and kept mixing other chemical combinations in hopes of finding the ideal plastic to create the scope. Neither Harry nor anyone on his team realized what cyanoacrylate could do.

Nine years later, in 1951, Harry was overseeing research at the Eastman Kodak Company. He and his team were trying to find a heat-proof material that could cover a jet engine. One of his team members, Fred Joyner, came to him with cyanoacrylate, something that he had just created on his own in the lab. Fred noted the stickiness of the product and that it became sticky just from one drop of water. Fred knew it was not the answer they were looking for, but this time he was more open-minded - he believed the product had potential for some kind of use.

When the product dried, it created a very tight bond. In fact, the bond was so tight it was almost unbreakable. Harry observed it could be used on wood, paper, and even human skin. (Today it is still used by medics on soldiers wounded in battle and by doctors for patients in hospitals.) Harry convinced Eastman Kodak to sell it to the public, and Kodak marketed the glue as Eastman #910 beginning in 1958. Eastman Kodak soon leased the rights to Loctite, who sold it to consumers as Loctite Quickset 404. Both companies eventually changed the name they called the product. You likely know them by names that are much easier to remember than Eastman #910 and Loctite Quickset 404 - and certainly easier to remember than "cyanoacrylate" . . . **Super Glue** and **Super Bond,** respectively.

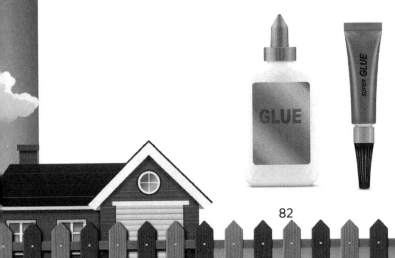

36: A Career to Dye For

What do you want to be when you grow up?

You have probably heard that question a hundred times. I think I have heard it at least once a year since first grade. People ask us the question so that we can set some goals for ourselves so that we can get to where we want to go. (By the way, it is okay to change your mind as you learn about new opportunities.)

William Perkin is a person who changed his mind about what he wanted to do. For several years, William wanted to find a cure for malaria, a common disease in many parts of the world in 1856. He pursued his goal with all his heart. By the time he was a teenager, he was already using a chemistry set to experiment daily to try to find the right combination of chemicals to cure malaria. One day he mixed tree bark and coal tar; sadly, he acknowledged that was not the cure. He was going to dump the thick purple sludge that resulted from the mixture but stopped himself – the sludge was a beautiful color. Might there be a use for it?

Dyes have been popular since early civilization. Squashed berries were among the first natural dyes. Even today, dyes are applied to hair and eggs at Easter; the most common use for dyes both then and now is for clothing. Clothing has been dyed to enhance its beauty, to enhance its usefulness such as in the case of camouflage, and to show rank such as royalty wearing purple.

William had just found a way to create a dye that was not found in nature. From that day on he was no longer interested in finding the cure for malaria; his new goal was to learn about the color he had created - he called it "mauve" - and to create a business selling it as a dye. William met his goals. He was soon able to isolate the pigment. By doing so, he became the first person to create an artificial dye, a dye not found in nature.

Soon other scientists found other colors. William and these other scientists saved numerous rare and endangered plants by replacing them with abundant man-made dyes. Also, with the colors readily available, the price of clothing fell. Today, we call these unnatural dyes, dyes not found in nature . . . **synthetic dyes.**

84

37: "Daddy! Daddy! Guess What?"

"Daddy! Daddy! Guess what?"

Have you ever said those words before? I have, and then I proceeded to tell him about whatever wonderment I just saw. My parents usually act interested and nod in understanding, recalling their own sense of wonderment when they were my age. Occasionally, I will share something they have never seen or heard of before, and then they become truly interested.

Dr. Washington Sheffield was a typical parent. He was a dentist in New London, Connecticut in 1890. His son had just gotten back from Paris, France where he had seen all types of strange sights, and he was sharing his adventures with his dad. (Any time one visits another culture, one comes to realize the people in that culture do not do all things the same way they are done in one's own culture.) One of the unique things that had intrigued his son was that in Paris the artists he saw painting did not use pallets of paint as they did in the United States; they used tubes. They would simply squirt out the amount of paint they needed, recap the tube, and keep the rest of the paint safe.

As he listened about the paint in the tube, Dr. Sheffield wondered if toothpaste could be put in such a tube. At that time, a family had a jar of toothpaste, and, when ready to brush their teeth, each person would moisten the brush bristles, dip the brush into the jar, and remove a small glob of toothpaste. Dr. Sheffield believed this was unsanitary. Dr. Sheffield had his own brand of toothpaste, Créme Dentifrice, so he decided to market it in tubes.

People liked the idea, and soon Colgate, a leading national toothpaste brand, was using the packaging technique as well. The first tubes were metal, but, when there was a metal shortage in the 1940s because of World War II, the tubes began to be made with plastic as well, and, in recent days, they are made completely of plastic. Also, caps used to unscrew, but many are now flip-top so that the cap does not roll away. Dentists recommend you use this product three times a day, so you have likely seen this accidental discovery . . . **the toothpaste tube.**

38: Human Nature's Curiosity Meets Mother Nature's Burdocks

Did you realize that a little thing like walking a dog could lead to a great invention? It happened to George de Mestral.

George was an electrical engineer who lived in Sweden. He decided to take his dog for a walk in the woods one chilly day in 1941. When he got back to his house, he noticed that burdock seeds he had brushed up against while walking in the woods were clinging to his coat; he also noticed that the burrs were on his dog's fur as well. This inspired George to think – how do those burdock seeds stick?

Just to look at them, he couldn't tell, so he got out a microscope. Upon closer examination, he noticed that the burdock seeds had little burrs that connected to the space between the threads of fabric in his coat; they had little hooks at the end of the burr that was able to connect to the little loops in his clothing. Fascinated with how the burrs fastened themselves so tightly, he then made a strip of miniature hooks that could snap into another strip with miniature loops. Just like the burr could be removed from his coat and reinserted, the hooks could be removed from the fabric and reinserted later. George saw potential for this fastener of hooks, and he patented the fastener in 1955.

George had originally used cotton in his product but found that nylon and polyester worked much better. He named the product "velvet hook." In the late 1950s, George began to sell the product. Today, the product is used to hang pictures on the wall, to close briefcases, and even to keep astronaut's pens from floating around in outer-space. You may never have heard of the "velvet hook" because George chose to use the French words "velour crochet" for "velvet hook;" in English we pronounce his invention as . . . **"Velcro."**

Do you use your own personal shorthand when taking notes? I know I do. For instance, I love to collect Knock-Knock Jokes, but rather than write out Knock-Knock by the joke, I save time by writing "KK." When I am in a hurry to find a Knock-Knock Joke, I simply scan the page for "KK."# Although no one else may be able to understand my shorthand, I can readily read it.

Norm Larson was a researcher in San Diego, California in 1953 looking for a way to keep water off Atlas missiles; if water got on the missiles, it caused them to rust and made them ineffective. The missiles were used as a deterrent - a notice to any nation that if it attacked the United States then its people would be attacked back. Norm knew that if rust were seen on the missile, it could signal weakness in the ability to counterattack and possibly invite an attack. Norm and his two associates knew their work was important for national security. They tried and tried to find the right combination of lubricants to prevent the rust, and time after time they failed. After thirty-nine failed attempts, they finally found a blend of oils that worked to displace water and prevent rust.

The product worked so well, that Larson began his own company, Rocket. He had seven employees at the time. A couple of the employees believed in the product a little too much – they snuck it home in their lunchbox to use around the house. Norm realized the product could be used for much more than just the aerospace industry, and, beginning in 1973, he began to bottle it in aerosol cans to sell to the general public. Today, his product is used around the house and in industry in literally hundreds of ways, from lubricating door hinges to unsticking rusted padlocks.

You may be wondering what the name of this accidental invention is. Recall that Norm was a research scientist looking for a way to prevent rust. He kept detailed records of his experiments so he could refer to them. In his notebook, he recorded each trial. He was careful to indicate where one attempt ended and the next began. At the beginning of each new experiment, he wrote the purpose of the experiment – "WD" for "Water Displacement" - and placed the trial number behind it. For instance, the first research trial was "WD-1". He decided to name the product the name that he had for it in his notebook . . . **WD-40.**

40: The Truth Will Come Out in the Wash

    I do some things that drive my parents crazy. For instance, I am tall for my age, so when my team needs a yard or two in a backyard American-style football game, they give the ball to me and I stretch forward. Needless to say, my knees are full of grass stains and dirt. Also, with my mother's permission, I have been known to jump in a mud puddle and splash mud all over myself. I will admit that at the end of most days, my clothes are gross and disgusting.

    Somehow, though, my parents do a miracle, and a few days later my clothes are returned from the clothes hamper to me as good as new. All the stains are gone. Thank goodness for laundry soap.

Laundry soap is something that we take for granted, but it has not always been around. Primitive people used to go to the river and try to beat the stains out of the clothing fibers with rocks. Laundry soap has gone through a lot of evolutionary changes in human history.

One of the places with extremely gross laundry is the hospital. I could joke with you about the grease stains from the fried chicken in the cafeteria, but that is not the only issue – most surgeons get lots of blood and bodily fluids on them. The next time they greet a patient before operating, though, they need to have germ-free, completely clean clothes. Doctors tend to wear white coats, and even a little stain can cause someone to question how clean the doctor keeps himself and his operating room. Someone had to come up with a chemical that could remove the toughest of stains unlike ordinary detergents – and the German company Henkel did just that in the 1960s.

The detergent worked so well that employees started to use it at home. (I don't encourage you to take from your employer without asking their permission; don't even take office supplies like pens and paper.) With or without permission, though, people started using this laundry soap at home - and they claimed it worked wonderful. That's when the manufacturer realized that with a couple of tweaks the product could be a residential cleaner. The company originally had no plans of creating a residential cleaner, but they suddenly realized they had accidentally discovered a household cleaner. You may even be wearing clothes cleaned by this cleaner which was originally designed just for hospitals; you are wearing them if your parents washed your clothes with . . . **Zout.**

CHAPTER THREE:

ACCIDENTAL DISCOVERY
OF
ITEMS OUTSIDE THE HOUSE

"Nearly all the great improvements, discoveries, inventions,
and achievements which have elevated and
blessed humanity have been the triumphs of enthusiasm."
~ Orison Swett Marden

41: Making the Cut

I love a good mystery. When someone has a bag or backpack, I always wonder what is in it. Typically, what is in the bag says a lot about the person. The same is true in days gone by as it is today. That said, did you know that doctors used to make house calls? That's right, instead of you going to the doctor, the doctor would come to you. When the doctor came, he - it was always a he in those days - would have a black bag with him full of tools and medicines. Have you ever wondered what was inside those bags? Would you believe me if I told you that one of the items in the bag was a chainsaw?

Believe it or not, the first chainsaw was invented by a doctor. It's not as gruesome as it sounds at first nor was it meant to frighten the patient. The doctor who invented the chainsaw was a Scottish surgeon, Bernhard Heine. Bernhard specialized in bone surgery. In the 1820s, doctors didn't have the tools that they have today, so a hammer and chisel were sometimes used. Heine wanted something less taxing on the body, so he invented a handheld device that had a long blade with a chain which had sharp teeth; the device had a handle with a crank and sprocket that turned the chain. He used the device like a drill to do brain surgery and also to help birth babies trapped in a mom's pelvis. He called his invention the "osteotome." and it is still used today for plastic surgery, dental surgery, and bone surgery.

John Muir, the Scottish-American naturalist who is regarded by many as the father of the United States national park system, saw the osteotome, and realized that the technology could be applied to the outdoors. He took the concept of the chain that sawed and applied it to cutting timber. Other people came along to make this wood-cutting device more portable and lighter, and they replaced the hand-crank with a gas or electric motor. Today, we know the invention as . . . **the chainsaw.**

42: Hurry, Hurry, Hurry

Here is your order

Many people at the beginning of the 1900s envisioned a world in which computers and cars would play a major role, and they pictured people having lots and lots of free time. They pictured both industries growing – and they did, but that free time they envisioned never came. If anything, we are busier today than people were then. We lead a very hectic life; a life that is full of go-go-go.

Businesses have tried to help us keep up the frantic pace. Back in 1900, if you wanted to go out to eat, you went to the restaurant, got out of your car or horse-and-buggy, and went inside to enjoy a meal. Jesse Kirby was a Dallas, Texas businessman who realized people didn't always have time to leave their cars, come inside, and enjoy the atmosphere of a restaurant. He created a restaurant, Kirby's Pig Stand, in September 1921 in which carhops would come to the car, get the order, and then bring the order out when it was done cooking. People could stay in their car, or, if they wanted, they could leave immediately upon receiving their food. (Jesse didn't really give them much of a choice about staying in their car; his restaurant did not have a dining room.)

Jesse's parking lot filled up with customers, but most stayed in the parking lot to eat rather than take the food with them. Jesse realized that if he could get the cars to move along, he could get a lot more sales. Jesse had an idea – an idea that would make him money and speed up service for the customers so they could move on with their hectic lives. Jesse implemented his idea in 1929 – Jesse let customers drive up to the kitchen window to order. This eliminated the carhop having to come out, making the ordering process faster. Once people got their food, they drove away as soon as they had their order, freeing up the space for the next customer.

His idea would be improved upon as technology advanced; for instance, intercoms are now standard in such lanes so people can order their food, and, by the time they get to the window, it can be ready. Unknown to Jesse, he had just invented the drive through lane and the drive through window.

To save space on signage, the fast-food industry has taught us not call it the "drive through lane" and "drive-through window"; they refer to the lane and the window as a unit and do not spell the words out completely. Instead of saying that Jesse invented the drive-through lane and drive-through window, we simply say that he invented . . . **the drive-thru.**

43: An Explosive Idea

Have you ever participated in a relay race in which you had to carry an egg on a spoon, walk to the other side of the room, walk back, and roll the egg onto your partner's spoon? If you dropped the egg, you had to start over with a new egg. I have done it, and it is not easy to walk quickly holding an egg on a spoon.

Now, pretend that egg is nitroglycerin. Nitroglycerin was an explosive more powerful than black powder in 1847; it was so powerful it could literally move a mountain. However, nitroglycerin was very touchy, and the slightest jolt could make it go off. If you thought carrying an egg was hard and had unwanted consequences, try carrying nitroglycerin.

Alfred Nobel realized if there was some way to cushion nitroglycerin, then it could be very useful. For instance, at this time steam railroads were becoming popular, and blasting a tunnel would be very helpful to both citizens along the route and profitable to the railroad company itself.

In 1863, Alfred invented the blasting cap. This allowed people to be far away from the nitroglycerin when it exploded; essentially, people lit a fuse from far away and waited for it to explode. This still did not resolve the issue of transporting the nitroglycerin to the site, though. Many people lost their lives trying to figure out how to transport it, including Alfred's brother Emil.

Alfred tried to make a bed for the nitroglycerin using sawdust, then coal, and then cement. Nothing worked. Alfred had some fossilized algae sitting on his desk, and he realized that crumpled earth – loosely packed dirt – might work. (Kitty litter looks and acts similar to this material.) He combined the nitroglycerin with a paste of the stabilizer and created "Nobel's Blasting Powder". He later became upset when he saw how people abused his invention and sought to use it for war and destruction, and he asked that 94% of his fortune be used to fund prizes that would promote peace, literature, economics and science – the Nobel Prize in these and other areas is given out each year if there are worthy recipients. You don't have to worry about the prize money running out anytime soon. Alfred made millions off "Nobel's Blasting Powder," a product he later renamed . . . **dynamite.**

44: The Invisible Became Visible

Have you ever heard of a white glove test? To make sure that something was clean, an inspector used to put on white gloves and run a finger down the surface of the item being inspected. Sadly – or perhaps fortunately – not everyone could pass a white glove inspection. Many times, things look clean but are not.

In 1978, someone left an invisible fingerprint on the table where Super Glue was being applied. A member of the Tokyo National Crime Lab happened to notice that the fumes from the Super Glue reacted with the moisture in the air and the acids in the fingerprint to create a white material that formed around the ridges of the previously invisible fingerprint.

Prior to this accidental invention of a new tool for a fingerprint kit, obvious fingerprints could be photographed, as could fingerprints that had been cast into an impressionable surface like mud, but invisible fingerprints could not be photographed. This new technology made invisible fingerprints visible, and now these fingerprints could be photographed. The Japanese shared the technology with the Americans who worked around them in the lab, and the technology quickly made its way to the United States.

No two people have the exact same fingerprints, so fingerprints are often essential to solving a crime. Detectives sometimes call the process of making these invisible prints visible as the Super Glue Method; crime lab techs use the fancy word cyanoacrylate fuming method to describe it; but the everyday person like me and you usually call it . . . **fingerprinting via fuming.**

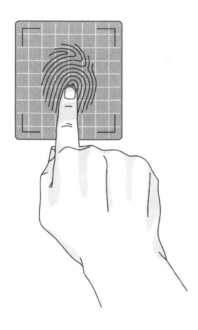

45: Devastation Provides Opportunities

Have you ever gotten to see the results of a natural disaster first-hand? In 2014, I was living in Charleston, South Carolina when a hurricane went through creating massive flooding. Entire buildings were underwater! I didn't see the hurricane; I had left town before it struck as the authorities advised. However, after the danger passed, the authorities let us back to our houses.

Going to see how things are after a natural disaster is human instinct. We want to access our environment. We want to see for ourselves what is happening. We want to determine what changes have taken place, to access the damage, and to decide how to move forward.

Primitive people had this same instinct. One day after a horrendous wildfire had passed through the forest, a group of men went into the charred woods to see what the situation was. One of them noticed that some animals had not made it out alive and that the fire had roasted them. Animals were hard to catch and too precious to waste, so the men gathered these charred animals to consume them. This was the first-time people had ever thought about eating cooked food; prior to that, everything they had eaten - plants or animals - had always been eaten raw. These men had just discovered cooked food.

Once a man noticed that one of the animals was not cooked thoroughly. He realized that if he put the animal back in the fire, he could cook it the rest of the way. This was the discovery of the art of cooking.

A smoldering branch was nearby, and the man realized that he could transport that smoldering branch and the fire it contained back to the camp; in other words, he did not have to cook the animal in the woods. He took the smoldering stick, got some kindling, and walked back to camp. This was the first instance of people being able to transport fire and of using it at the campsite.

Soon he had a flame going in the camp. The flame just had to be fed, but as long as the flame was fed, it would be there – in addition to providing a source of cooking, the flame provided light, it enhanced safety by scaring off wild animals, and it provided warmth. In time, people would also learn that it was a great way to mold one's tools.

You may never have thought of cooked meat or a controlled flame as an accidental invention, but people did not simply decide they wanted to cook – an accident led to it. In time, people would learn how to bang flint on a rock to create a spark that would ignite the flame. For numerous years, though, people had to rely on nature to initiate the flames.

What happened in the above story may have happened in a day or it may have happened over thousands of years, scientists aren't sure. What they do know, though, is that this is one of the greatest accidental discoveries, this flame that we call . . . **fire.**

46: Keeping Away Evil Spirits

I love my nightlight. My nightlight allows me to see what is in the room, but it is not so bright that I cannot sleep. Prior to having my nightlight, I used to hear all kinds of noises, pops, and creaks, and my imagination would run wild with images of the Bogey Man walking around the house, hiding in my closet, or crawling army-style under my bed. With my nightlight, though, I could readily tell that there was no Bogey Man about to attack me; I was reassured that the noise I heard was just a board expanding or shrinking as it reacted to the temperature.

The ancient Chinese had fears of Bogey Men too. They believed that evil spirits were all around them. They didn't have nightlights, but they did have bamboo shoots which they would toss into the fire to create a loud popping sound which they believed scared away the evil spirits. Evil spirits were thought to be everywhere, and so they would burn bamboo to create pops at weddings, funerals, religious rituals, and whenever they detected an evil spirit was nearby.

One day around the year 200, an unknown cook placed charcoal, sulfur, and saltpeter (potassium nitrate) over a fire, and the mixture exploded with a loud bang! The cook realized that this noise was even louder than the noise made from the bamboo. The cook decided to put bamboo shoots and powder together. He poured the mixture of charcoal, saltpeter, and sulfur into the bamboo shoot, tossed it into the fire, turned his back while holding his ears, and waited for the noise – Bang! He tried it again, this time with more powder, and the result was the same, only louder – BANG! This accidental invention of the magic powder inside the bamboo soon replaced the solo bamboo stick.

In the 1830s Italians took the accidental Chinese invention one step further. They realized that if certain chemicals were added to the mixture, then that the chemical could be seen as it burned in the sky. Different chemicals produced different colors – for instance, sulfur would burn yellow and barium would burn green. They created an aerial shell, added the powder, and then added the chemicals that would burn the desired color. Now the spectator not only heard the boom but also saw pretty colors light up the sky – and, sometimes when the color-producing chemicals burned, they even produced more noises for the spectator to enjoy.

Today we use these pretty but noisy devices for many celebrations, particularly on New Year's Celebration and Independence Day. They are also used for personal events, such as weddings. You may not be trying to scare off an evil spirit, but chances are you have seen this discovery . . . **firecrackers** – which was the original discovery consisting of the noise - and fireworks – which is the firecracker plus the pretty lights.

47: Pumped on Technology!

You have likely heard the riddle – which came first, the chicken or the egg? I have one for you – which came first, the automobile or the fuel pump?

If you said fuel pump, you were right. Believe it or not, the fuel pump was created long before the automobile became a common sight. Here is what happened:

In 1885 a general store owner in Fort Wayne, Indiana, was tired of both the smell and the mess kerosene made in his store. He could not discontinue selling kerosene though. Kerosene was profitable for him and a necessity for his customer - customers used kerosene in their lamps so they could see and, in their stoves, so they had heat. At that time, kerosene was kept in a barrel and had to be ladled out into the customer's container. This took valuable time and caused the employees to smell of kerosene – not the smell the store owner wanted to have carried around his grocery items. One day he asked Sylvanus Bowser – "S.F. Bowser; the "F" stood for Freelove – to invent a machine that would suck kerosene from barrels so the kerosene could be conveniently placed in a customer's portable can. Bowser succeeded. He came up with a machine that would tap into the barrel. Each crank of the pump resulted in one gallon of kerosene being poured into the customer's container.

Although Bowser intended for his invention to dispense kerosene, in the 1890s Bowser realized that his pump was capable of delivering gasoline to the increasingly common automobile, so he tweaked it, adding a hose and, eventually, a nozzle. The machine would have numerous minor tweaks over the years to make it more accurate and to better filter the fuel. To this day, in some places around the world, the pump that dispenses fuel is called "Bowser" after the inventor. It is also known as the petrol pump and the gas pump, but you probably know it as . . . **the gasoline pump.**

48: A Cold-War Shell Game

Have you ever tried to hide something from your brothers and sisters - and then forgotten where you placed it? I've done it many times.

In the middle of the Cold War, the United States did not have a lot of missiles, and so, what few it did have it would move around the country. By doing this moving, the United States believed the enemy countries would not know exactly where the missiles were at any time; this made them harder to target and harder still to verify they had been destroyed. The United States moved the missiles by train from one location to another using ordinary railroad freight cars. The freight car carrying the missiles looked exactly like the other freight cars. To keep the missiles' whereabouts a secret, very few people knew where the missiles were at any time.

If you have ever watched a con artist place a marble under one of a possible three shells and then move the shells around rapidly, you understand how the missile could be easily lost - this was exactly what the Air Force wanted to happen to the enemies' tracking, but, of course, the United States Air Force itself needed to know where the missile was at all times.

Ivan Getting, the Vice President for engineering and research at the Raytheon Corporation in 1951, came up with a solution so the Air Force could keep track of the missile. He worked with the United States Air Force to strategically place 18 satellites into the sky. Just like the North Star was used by ancient sailors, these 18 satellites allowed people to calculate geographical positions within a few feet.

After the Cold War ended, the technology was used for peaceful purposes. Although no one had set out to create such a navigation system for cars and boats, this accidental invention changed the world of transportation. At first people had to buy the unit in stores if they wanted one, but, soon, the item came pre-installed in cars and in smartphones. People could beam a signal to the satellites to see where they were or to get step-by-step directions to get to their destination. This system of satellites and the device that works with them is called the Global Positioning System. You may not have heard it called that, but you have likely heard of . . . **the GPS.**

49: Fire Medicine

Have you ever heard your mom and dad say that they would like to be young again? For years people have searched for the Fountain of Youth; the quest for that fountain is one of the reasons Spanish explorers came to Florida in the 1500s. A magical fountain is just one idea of how to return to one's youth.

In China in 850, people thought that a potion could be created to make one young again. The aging king wanted to be young again, and so he asked two chemists to discover the magic formula. The chemists at that time believed that saltpeter – a combination of sulfur and potassium nitrate – was the key ingredient to create the formula, but they were clueless of what to add with the saltpeter. One day, the chemists decided to add birthwort herb to it along with some charcoal, and they were disappointed that nothing happened. They then decided to try to heat the mixture to see if that would produce the syrup for eternal life.

When they held the mixture over the fire, the mixture exploded. You have probably seen cartoons in which people have blackened faces and mussed up hair following an explosion; that is what happened to these gentlemen. It also created small fires in the laboratory that had to be put out. This mixture that was supposed to be life-giving almost instantly became life-taking.

The mixture created a force when it exploded, and the scientists realized that it could propel objects. The chemists saw potential in the product for the military. For instance, it could work like a rocket, propelling a flaming arrow onto enemy invaders. This invention propelled China into a regional powerhouse and led to other inventions, such as landmines, bombs, and flamethrowers. What was supposed to give life brought death.

What was this magic black powder that they had discovered? The Chinese called it "fire medicine." In English, "fire medicine" translates to . . . **gun powder.**

50: Science Fiction Became Reality

Have you ever seen the 1940s Superman cartoons in which speeding bullets bounce off the chest of Superman's uniform? Just like Dick Tracy's watch was a videophone long before videophones were created, Superman's bulletproof uniform was pure science fiction. (The citizens of Metropolis said he was the "man of steel", but if you look closely you will notice those bullets never penetrated his clothes to get to his skin – I don't have a doubt that he was wearing a suit made of bullet-proof material.)

Today, bullet-proof clothing is a reality. Believe it or not though, the person who invented it was not seeking to invent bullet-proof clothing – she was trying to invent a special car tire. Here is what happened:

In 1964, Stephanie Kwolek, an employee of Dupont, was trying to create a strong, lightweight car tire because Dupont anticipated an energy shortage coming and believed that lighter vehicles would make better use of what little fuel was available. At that time, tires had steel in them, and she was trying to find a substitute for the steel. What she found was a lightweight fabric that is five times stronger than steel. (For those interested in the science, it is five times stronger than steel because of how the molecules arrange themselves and form strong hydrogen bonds between the molecular chains.)

Her invention has been used to protect both police officers and soldiers, and the material can be found in planes, boats, cars, and other items. You have probably heard of bullet-proof clothing. For that matter, the same material is knife-proof as well. Because it protects one from more than bullets, the official term for the fabric is . . . **Kevlar.**

51: The Electric Broom

Have you ever hosed off a driveway? To do so, you take a garden hose, put your finger over the end of the hose to dam up the water and to build pressure, and then you aim the water at the grass clippings or whatever you want removed. It is an effective way to get the driveway clear of debris and sparkling clean.

But what If you were in a drought and it was against the law to use water to do that? If you wanted a clean driveway, what would you do? "Sweep it with a broom" is a great answer, and many people chose to do exactly that in California in 1950. Dom Quinto, though, found sweeping to be too much work.

Dom owned a chemical sprayer. The sprayer was a Japanese yard-work machine that had a backpack with a motor he could put on his back, a tank for chemicals that he could screw onto a hose that attached to the backpack, and an off-on switch that allowed the motor to push air over the reservoir and create a mist that coated his plants. The machine worked the opposite of a vacuum; instead of sucking air and dirt into the machine, this machine pushed air and chemicals out of it. Dom decided to remove the chemical tank and simply used the forced air to clean his driveway. Some would call Dom lazy; others would call him a genius.

Dom blew all the unwanted clutter off his driveway – grass clippings, pebbles, dust, sticks, and leaves. In time, the Japanese company would see that Dom and others did not use the chemical tank on their weed-killer spreader, and, in 1970, they would begin to create a tank-free product – basically a motor and a hose - that could blow driveways and yards clean. Because the product was mostly known for its ability to blow leaves, they called it . . . **the leaf blower.**

52: The Lazy Man

GOLD?

All right, I admit it. I am kind of lazy.

That's not necessarily a bad thing, though. If I can find an easier, more efficient way of doing something, I will likely do it that more efficient way than the way I am currently doing it. This has been common throughout human history.

Have you ever stood in front of the monkey cage at the zoo and gotten the attention of one of the captive primates? One of the games they will play with you is monkey-see-monkey-do. If you start to rub your stomach, the monkey will start to rub its stomach. If you start to scratch your head, the monkey will scratch its head. Monkey-see-money-do is how society works too. Because almost all of us are somewhat lazy, if we see an invention that works really well, we are likely to copy it. After it has been copied a few times, no one knows who the real founder is.

Let me tell you about one of the laziest men in history, but also one of the greatest accidental inventors. The man lived thousands of years ago in Mesopotamia or Egypt. This man's entire generation was already considered lazy by his grandparents because his entire generation refused to wander around for food but instead, they had learned to farm - they simply planted the seeds and waited for the food to come to them. This particular man was even lazier than his friends; not only didn't he like to wander; he also didn't even like to bend over to pick up piles of dried grass or grains. He was so lazy that he picked up a two-pronged stick that had fallen from a tree at the edge of the field and used it to lift the grass off the ground and set it on the pile.

His friends watched him as he effortlessly lifted the grain without stooping. They too got two-pronged sticks. Soon, the two-pronged stick was considered a basic tool in farming. Over the years, people standardized a handle on the stick and added another two or more tongs. Once people knew how to forge iron, they began to create the tines out of iron because the wood tines broke easily.

The modern version of this device has two to five tines and a long handle. It is used on the farm to lift hay, leaves, and other loose materials. (It's offspring, a shorter device with thicker tines is called the garden fork. The dinner fork can also trace its roots to this invention.) Like many inventions, this one is just a re-creation of something that already existed in nature. This fork that pitches hay and other materials is aptly named; we call it . . . **the pitchfork.**

53: Fifty Buckets of Gold Coming Up – I Hope

Do you want to be rich? Lots of people do. Money may not be the secret to happiness, but we all like nice things. Also, we need some degree of money just to survive.

If you thought that you could turn your urine into gold, would you start to save your urine? A German scientist named Henning Brand did exactly that. He collected over 50 buckets of his urine and placed them in the cellar under his house. (And you thought your mom and dad kept some funky things in the cellar.) He believed that after a few months, the urine would turn to gold.

Now, before you write this guy off as the weirdest neighbor ever, let's remember that this was 1699. In those days, shampoo was not invented, so people often used urine to wash their hair. Also, urine was also used to dye clothing. Henning was not the only person to have a bucket of urine in his cellar. (He may have been the only one to have 50 buckets, though, or the only one who expected something like the Gold Fairy to come by and turn them into gold.)

He was disappointed when he went down several months later and saw that he was surrounded by fermented urine and no gold. Frustrated but still believing he could make gold from urine, he boiled away the liquid. This left a paste, which he then heated to a high temperature. He hoped he would find gold – but he didn't.

What he found instead is a chemical that appears in human bones. He and others soon found that the material was very useful as a fertilizer, detergent, and pesticide. He observed a glow to the white material when it mixed with oxygen, so he named it the Greek term for "light bearer" . . . **phosphorus.**

54: Rain, Rain, Go Away

Isn't it frustrating when you have something planned that you want to do that involves sunlight and all the weather does for days at a time is be overcast and rainy?

You aren't the only one to feel that way. Henri Becquerel was a French scientist, and he had a great idea he wanted to try. He had read about the recently discovered x-ray invention, and he thought It might be possible to make x-rays from the sun. He thought he could catch the sunlight with uranium salts and then generate x-rays which would then cause the photographic plates to show a picture. As most scientists do, he wanted to run a test to see if he was right. When the sun didn't shine, he knew he had to wait for another day, so he put the photographic plate and the uranium salts in a desk drawer so they wouldn't get lost.

Some researchers are penny-pinchers, and Henri was one of those. After days of no sun, he realized that he would need to create a new photographic plate. Not wanting to miss a chance to hone his skills with developing photo plates, he decided to practice his developing skills on this photographic plate before pitching it. He was expecting a completely black sheet to result, but when he developed it, to his amazement he found the film had been exposed – but how; it was away from light in the desk drawer. He quickly suspected the uranium; he suspected and later proved the uranium was giving out invisible radiation. It was the radiation from the uranium that had caused the image on the photographic plate.

Today both x-rays and Henri's discovery are used in hospitals, doctors' offices, and dentists' offices for both detecting problems, such as having someone swallow a dye so doctors can see what happens inside the person, and for fixing problems, such as using lasers to attack cancer cells. Today, we call the energy that uranium gives off . . . **radiation.**

55: The Shattered Flask

Have you ever walked by and knocked something off the counter or table? I am embarrassed to admit it, but I've knocked down my mom's vase from the living room table as well as knocked drinking glasses off the kitchen counter. Thanks to gravity pulling these fragile items down so hard, they tend to break when they hit the floor – and my mom is not happy.

Adults knock things down too. Take Edouard Benedictus, for example. Edouard Benedictus has gone down in history for his clumsiness. One day in 1903, Edouard was climbing a ladder in his science lab to get a chemical when he accidentally knocked over a flask from a shelf below. As anyone would expect, gravity pulled the item to the ground as a horrified, helpless Edouard could merely look on.

However, here is where the unexpected enters the story. Edouard looked down at the floor, expecting to see the flask in thousands of small pieces and shards of glass scattered throughout the room, but instead the flask just had a small crack in it. How could this be, he wondered?

He then recalled what was in the flask the last time he used it – cellulose nitrate. Apparently, his assistant had gotten lazy with washing the equipment, and a thin coating of the cellulose nitrate was still coating the flask. Edouard concluded the cellulose nitrate prevented the glass from breaking. He thought of many uses for his new product, including installing it in automobiles. The military had ideas too, using it in gas masks in World War I. Edouard called his discovery "laminated glass", but others have called it "shatter-proof glass", "bullet-proof glass", and, the one you have likely heard it called, . . . **safety glass.**

Did you enjoy the book?

If you did, we are ecstatic. If not, please write your complaint to us and we will ensure to fix it.

If you're feeling generous, there is something important that you can help me with – tell other people that you enjoyed the book.

Ask a grown-up to write about it on Amazon. When they do, more people will find out about the book. It also lets Amazon know that we are making kids around the world laugh. Even a few words and ratings would go a long way.

If you have any ideas or jokes that you think are super funny, please let us know. We would love to hear from you. Our email address is -

riddleland@riddlelandforkids.com

Riddleland Bonus

Join our Facebook Group at
Riddleland For Kids to get daily jokes and riddles.

Bonus Book

https://pixelfy.me/riddlelandbonus

Thank you for buying this book. As a token of our appreciation, we would like to offer a special bonus—a collection of 50 original jokes, riddles, and funny stories.

Other Fun Books By Riddleland
Riddles Series

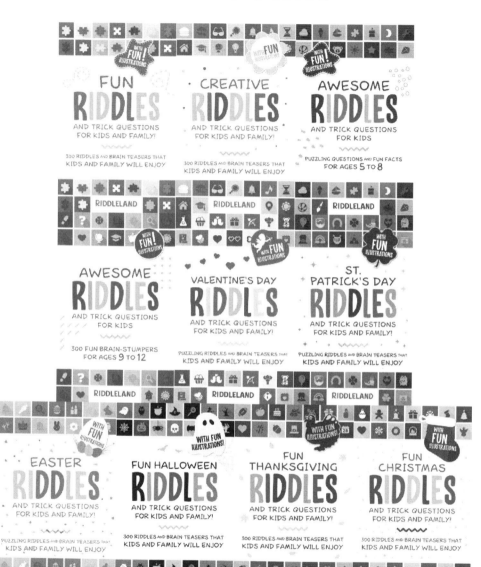

FUN RIDDLES AND TRICK QUESTIONS FOR KIDS AND FAMILY!
300 RIDDLES AND BRAIN TEASERS THAT KIDS AND FAMILY WILL ENJOY

CREATIVE RIDDLES AND TRICK QUESTIONS FOR KIDS AND FAMILY!
300 RIDDLES AND BRAIN TEASERS THAT KIDS AND FAMILY WILL ENJOY

AWESOME RIDDLES AND TRICK QUESTIONS FOR KIDS
PUZZLING QUESTIONS AND FUN FACTS FOR AGES 5 TO 8

AWESOME RIDDLES AND TRICK QUESTIONS FOR KIDS
300 FUN BRAIN-STUMPERS FOR AGES 9 TO 12

VALENTINE'S DAY RIDDLES AND TRICK QUESTIONS FOR KIDS AND FAMILY!
PUZZLING RIDDLES AND BRAIN TEASERS THAT KIDS AND FAMILY WILL ENJOY

ST. PATRICK'S DAY RIDDLES AND TRICK QUESTIONS FOR KIDS AND FAMILY!
PUZZLING RIDDLES AND BRAIN TEASERS THAT KIDS AND FAMILY WILL ENJOY

EASTER RIDDLES AND TRICK QUESTIONS FOR KIDS AND FAMILY!
PUZZLING RIDDLES AND BRAIN TEASERS THAT KIDS AND FAMILY WILL ENJOY

FUN HALLOWEEN RIDDLES AND TRICK QUESTIONS FOR KIDS AND FAMILY!
300 RIDDLES AND BRAIN TEASERS THAT KIDS AND FAMILY WILL ENJOY

FUN THANKSGIVING RIDDLES AND TRICK QUESTIONS FOR KIDS AND FAMILY!
300 RIDDLES AND BRAIN TEASERS THAT KIDS AND FAMILY WILL ENJOY

FUN CHRISTMAS RIDDLES AND TRICK QUESTIONS FOR KIDS AND FAMILY!
300 RIDDLES AND BRAIN TEASERS THAT KIDS AND FAMILY WILL ENJOY

Its Laugh O'Clock Joke Books

It's Laugh O'Clock Would You Rather Books

Get them on Amazon
or our website at www.riddlelandforkids.com

About Riddleland

Riddleland is a mum + dad run publishing company. We are passionate about creating fun and innovative books to help children develop their reading skills and fall in love with reading. If you have suggestions for us or want to work with us, shoot us an email at

riddleland@riddlelandforkids.com

Our family's favorite quote:

"Creativity is an area in which younger people
have a tremendous advantage since
they have an endearing habit of always
questioning past wisdom and authority."
~ Bill Hewlett

REFERENCES

40 history: Learn the stories behind the wd-40 Brand. (n.d.). Retrieved April 05, 2021, from https://www.wd40.com/history/

54 explosive facts about Fireworks. (n.d.). Retrieved April 05, 2021, from https://www.factretriever.com/firework-facts

About scotch® BRAND. (n.d.). Retrieved April 02, 2021, from https://www.scotchbrand.com/3M/en_US/scotch-brand/about/

About splenda. (2020, August 11). Retrieved April 02, 2021, from https://www.splenda.com/about-splenda/

About us. (n.d.). Retrieved April 02, 2021, from https://enchroma.com/pages/about-us

Accidental discoveries in science. (2018, June 14). Retrieved April 02, 2021, from https://raed.academy/en/accidental-discoveries-science/

Accidental inventions and the story behind archimedes' eureka. (2020, October 21). Retrieved April 05, 2021, from https://www.knowledgestuff.com/accidental-inventions/

Admin. (2016, November 20). Sandwich facts: 25 interesting facts about sandwiches. Retrieved April 02, 2021, from https://www.kickassfacts.com/25-interesting-facts-about-sandwiches/

Admin. (2019, September 19). The sweet history of iced tea. Retrieved April 02, 2021, from https://www.revolutiontea.com/blogs/news/the-sweet-history-of-iced-tea

Begley, S. (2015, September 03). The history of the tea bag. Retrieved April 02, 2021, from https://time.com/3996712/a-brief-history-of-the-tea-bag/

Bellis, M. (n.d.). Alfred Nobel was the inventor of this explosive substance. Retrieved April 05, 2021, from https://www.thoughtco.com/history-of-dynamite-1991564

Bellis, M. (n.d.). Biography of Thomas Adams, American inventor. Retrieved April 02, 2021, from https://www.thoughtco.com/thomas-adams-and-history-of-chewing-gum-4075422

Bellis, M. (n.d.). How much do you know about the history and invention of wd-40? Retrieved April 05, 2021, from https://www.thoughtco.com/wd-40-1992659

Bellis, M. (n.d.). Learn about the history of the gps. Retrieved April 05, 2021, from https://www.thoughtco.com/history-of-the-global-positioning-system-1991853

Bellis, M. (n.d.). Learn how mother nature became the inspiration behind velcro. Retrieved April 05, 2021, from https://www.thoughtco.com/who-invented-velcro-4019660

Bellis, M. (n.d.). Meet the BANJO-PLAYING engineer who INVENTED scotch tape. Retrieved April 02, 2021, from https://www.thoughtco.com/history-of-scotch-tape-1992403

Bellis, M. (n.d.). Pepsi Cola's long, Winding History. Retrieved April 02, 2021, from https://www.thoughtco.com/history-of-pepsi-cola-1991656

Bellis, M. (n.d.). Sewing is a lot safer thanks to this inventor. Retrieved April 02, 2021, from https://www.thoughtco.com/walter-hunt-profile-1991916

Bellis, M. (n.d.). The invention of scotchgard patsy sherman. Retrieved April 02, 2021, from http://www.theinventors.org/library/inventors/blscotchgard.htm

Bellis, M. (n.d.). Where did kevlar body armor come from? Retrieved April 05, 2021, from https://www.thoughtco.com/history-of-kevlar-stephanie-kwolek-4076518

Bernstein, N. (2013, February 07). Accidental science. Retrieved April 05, 2021, from https://sites.psu.edu/passion2bernstein/2013/02/07/fireworks/

Bernstein, N. (2013, March 22). Accidental science. Retrieved April 05, 2021, from https://sites.psu.edu/passion2bernstein/2013/03/22/safety-glass/

The best accidental inventions. (2019, March 29). Retrieved April 05, 2021, from https://inventionland.com/storytelling/the-best-accidental-inventions/

Bob Switzer. (2020, December 30). Retrieved April 02, 2021, from https://en.wikipedia.org/wiki/Bob_Switzer

Bouffard, B. (2016, June 15). Inventor of the month - who IS EDOUARD BENEDICTUS? Retrieved April 05, 2021, from https://innovate-design.com/inventor-month-edouard-benedictus/

A brief history of licorice candy. (2020, April 17). Retrieved April 02, 2021, from https://www.candyclub.com/blog/history-of-licorice-candy/

A brief history of the tea bag. (n.d.). Retrieved April 02, 2021, from http://www.patentlyinteresting.com/history-of-the-tea-bag.html

Butler, S. (2014, July 18). The story of the sandwich. Retrieved April 02, 2021, from https://www.history.com/news/the-story-of-the-sandwich

Chewing gum. (2021, March 10). Retrieved April 02, 2021, from https://en.wikipedia.org/wiki/Chewing_gum

Chimichanga. (2021, March 28). Retrieved April 02, 2021, from https://en.wikipedia.org/wiki/Chimichanga

Chowhound. (n.d.). Who really invented sloppy joes? Retrieved April 02, 2021, from https://www.chowhound.com/food-news/202832/who-really-invented-sloppy-joes/

Control of fire by early humans. (2021, March 25). Retrieved April 05, 2021, from https://en.wikipedia.org/wiki/Control_of_fire_by_early_humans

Crow, S. (2020, February 21). 15 things you don't know About Pepperidge Farm. Retrieved April 02, 2021, from https://www.eatthis.com/pepperidge-farm-cookie-facts/

Crêpes Suzette. (2020, August 19). Retrieved April 02, 2021, from https://en.wikipedia.org/wiki/Cr%C3%AApes_Suzette

Cyanoacrylate (super glue) fuming. (n.d.). Retrieved April 05, 2021, from http://www.personal.psu.edu/msp5018/blogs/english_202c/the-development-of-fingerprints-with-cyanoacrylate-super-glue-fuming.html

The cyanoacrylate fuming method - science olympiad. (n.d.). Retrieved April 5, 2021, from https://www.soinc.org/sites/default/files/uploaded_files/forensics/For_supergluing.pdf

Deutan (DEUTERANOMALY). (n.d.). Retrieved April 02, 2021, from https://enchroma.com/pages/deutan

Dickinson, K. (2019, September 12). The invention that made us human: Fire. Retrieved April 05, 2021, from https://bigthink.com/surprising-science/inventions-fire

Dippin'dots: Curt JONES. (2019, September 09). Retrieved April 02, 2021, from https://www.npr.org/2019/09/06/758394062/dippin-dots-curt-jones

Dry cleaning. (2021, March 17). Retrieved April 02, 2021, from https://en.wikipedia.org/wiki/Dry_cleaning

Dynamite - history of dynamite. (n.d.). Retrieved April 05, 2021, from https://www.softschools.com/inventions/history/dynamite_history/370/

Dynamite. (2021, March 23). Retrieved April 05, 2021, from https://en.wikipedia.org/wiki/Dynamite

Engelbrecht, K. (n.d.). The story BEHIND Dutch drop, A licorice love affair. Retrieved April 02, 2021, from https://www.thespruceeats.com/the-netherlands-love-for-licorice-1128579

Eschner, K. (2016, December 15). Ever wonder who invented the tea bag? Retrieved April 02, 2021, from https://www.smithsonianmag.com/smart-news/ever-wonder-who-invented-tea-bag-180961469/

The evolution of bullet resistant glass. (2020, January 02). Retrieved April 05, 2021, from https://www.tssbulletproof.com/blog/the-evolution-of-bullet-resistant-glass/

The facts about your FAVORITE Beverages (U.S.): HOME. (n.d.). Retrieved April 02, 2021, from https://www.pepsicobeveragefacts.com/

Falkowitz, M. (2019, May 10). Who invented the chimichanga? Retrieved April 02, 2021, from https://www.tastecooking.com/who-invented-the-chimichanga/

Feverfew. (n.d.). Retrieved April 02, 2021, from https://www.nccih.nih.gov/health/feverfew

Filippone, P. (n.d.). The interesting origin and history of worcestershire sauce. Retrieved April 02, 2021, from https://www.thespruceeats.com/worcestershire-sauce-history-1807686

Fireworks. (2021, April 04). Retrieved April 05, 2021, from https://en.wikipedia.org/wiki/Fireworks

Flash freezing. (2020, December 14). Retrieved April 02, 2021, from https://en.wikipedia.org/wiki/Flash_freezing

Food articles, News & features section. (n.d.). Retrieved April 02, 2021, from https://www.foodreference.com/html/a-crepes-suzette.html

Food articles, News & features section. (n.d.). Retrieved April 05, 2021, from http://www.foodreference.com/html/art-history-fork-729.html

Fountain of youth. (2021, February 13). Retrieved April 05, 2021, from https://en.wikipedia.org/wiki/Fountain_of_Youth

Ganninger, D. (2020, December 17). What does wd-40 stand for? Retrieved April 05, 2021, from https://medium.com/knowledge-stew/what-does-wd-40-stand-for-b884a91e8923

Gasoline pump. (2021, March 26). Retrieved April 05, 2021, from https://en.wikipedia.org/wiki/Gasoline_pump

Gershenson, G. (2021, March 29). A brief and bizarre history of artificial sweeteners. Retrieved April 02, 2021, from https://www.saveur.com/artificial-sweeteners/

Gershenson, G. (2021, March 29). A brief and bizarre history of artificial sweeteners. Retrieved April 02, 2021, from https://www.saveur.com/artificial-sweeteners/

Goodrich, R. (2013, May 21). Who invented Velcro? Retrieved April 05, 2021, from https://www.livescience.com/34572-velcro.html

Grossman, D. (2017, November 14). The serendipitous history of superglue. Retrieved April 02, 2021, from https://www.popularmechanics.com/technology/a25067/the-surprising-military-history-of-superglue/

Gunpowder. (2021, March 31). Retrieved April 05, 2021, from https://en.wikipedia.org/wiki/Gunpowder

Hartley, J. (2008, April 28). Nutrasweet - the history of this toxic chemical and its Promotion (part 1). Retrieved April 02, 2021, from https://www.organicconsumers.org/news/nutrasweet-history-toxic-chemical-and-its-promotion-part-1

Helmenstine, A., Ph.D. (n.d.). How firework colors work and the chemicals that make vivid colors. Retrieved April 05, 2021, from https://www.thoughtco.com/chemistry-of-firework-colors-607341

Henri Becquerel. (1852, December 15). Retrieved April 05, 2021, from https://www.atomicheritage.org/profile/henri-becquerel

Hirst, K. (n.d.). When did people begin using fire? Retrieved April 05, 2021, from https://www.thoughtco.com/the-discovery-of-fire-169517

History - wd-40 company. (2020, July 21). Retrieved April 05, 2021, from https://www.wd40company.com/our-company/our-history/

The history And Collectability of gas pumps. (2020, September 03). Retrieved April 05, 2021, from https://www.automobiledrivingmuseum.org/the-history-and-collectability-of-gas-pumps/

The history and evolution of chainsaws. (n.d.). Retrieved April 5, 2021, from https://chainsawcarvinghistory.com/history-of-chainsaws/

History and story behind inventions: Toothpaste tube. (n.d.). Retrieved April 5, 2021, from https://www.trivia-library.com/a/history-and-story-behind-inventions-toothpaste-tube.htm

The history behind your tube of toothpaste. (n.d.). Retrieved April 05, 2021, from https://www.deardoctor.com/dentistry/blog/history-behind-your-tube-of-toothpaste

History of gunpowder. (2021, March 30). Retrieved April 05, 2021, from https://en.wikipedia.org/wiki/History_of_gunpowder

The history of high-vis clothing. (2020, February 13). Retrieved April 02, 2021, from https://www.prudentialuniforms.com/blog/history-high-vis-clothing/

The history of iced tea. (2018, April 30). Retrieved April 02, 2021, from https://www.teasource.com/blogs/beyond-the-leaf/he-history-of-iced-tea

HISTORY OF SACCHARIN. (n.d.). Retrieved April 02, 2021, from https://saccharin.org/history/

History of super glue - facts about super glue. (n.d.). Retrieved April 02, 2021, from http://www.gluehistory.com/glue-rigin/history-of-super-glue/

The history of the leaf blower. (n.d.). Retrieved April 05, 2021, from https://es.scribd.com/document/59045387/The-History-of-the-Leaf-Blower

History of the tarte tatin. (n.d.). Retrieved April 02, 2021, from http://www.tartetatin.org/home/history-of-the-tarte-tatin

A history of the world - object : Worcestershire sauce. (n.d.). Retrieved April 02, 2021, from http://www.bbc.co.uk/ahistoryoftheworld/objects/mcraSW4BRJyBTtOMbcb6Tw

History of tofu. (n.d.). Retrieved April 02, 2021, from https://www.chodangtofu.com/history.html

History of yogurt. (n.d.). Retrieved April 02, 2021, from http://www.indepthinfo.com/yogurt/history.htm

Hitt, C. (n.d.). The highly caffeinated & Super-interesting history of Mountain Dew. Retrieved April 02, 2021, from https://www.thrillist.com/news/nation/history-of-mountain-dew-origin-facts

How did scotch tape appear and what is the story behind its name? (n.d.). Retrieved April 02, 2021, from https://all-spares.com/en/articles-and-video/how-did-scotch-tape-appear-and-what-is-the-story-behind-its-name.html

HOW WE MAID HISTORY. (n.d.). Retrieved April 02, 2021, from http://maid-rite.com/history.php

Howard, K. (2018, March 01). The totally Gross tale of how Pink lemonade got its color. Retrieved April 02, 2021, from https://allthatsinteresting.com/pink-lemonade-origins

The Icee Company. (2021, March 04). Retrieved April 02, 2021, from https://en.wikipedia.org/wiki/The_Icee_Company
Inflation rate between 1635-2021: Inflation calculator. (n.d.). Retrieved April 02, 2021, from https://www.in2013dollars.com/us/inflation

Invention of gunpowder. (2020, May 27). Retrieved April 05, 2021, from https://severnhistoricalsociety.org/timeline/invention-of-gunpowder/

Ivory (soap). (2021, March 26). Retrieved April 02, 2021, from https://en.wikipedia.org/wiki/Ivory_(soap)

Izon, J. (2020, July 13). What are Dippin' Dots, Really? The history of Cryogenic ice cream. Retrieved April 02, 2021, from https://www.seriouseats.com/2020/07/dippin-dots-history-mini-melts.html

Jack, J. (2021, January 31). History of leaf Blowers. Retrieved April 05, 2021, from https://leafblowersguide.com/history-of-leaf-blowers/

John Muir. (2012, February 17). Retrieved April 05, 2021, from https://www.californiamuseum.org/inductee/john-muir

John Walker (inventor). (2021, February 21). Retrieved April 02, 2021, from https://en.wikipedia.org/wiki/John_Walker_(inventor)

John Walker - inventor of the FRICTION MATCH. (n.d.). Retrieved April 02, 2021, from http://www.historyofmatches.com/matches-inventors/john-walker/

Jung, T. (2020, January 17). The history of reflective material. Retrieved April 02, 2021, from https://www.jungkwang.com/post/the-history-of-reflective-material

K. (2014, February 11). The 10 most POPULAR accidental inventions. Retrieved April 02, 2021, from https://www.therichest.com/most-popular/the-10-most-popular-accidental-inventions/

Kazek, K. (2020, August 12). A history of Mountain Dew: FROM HILLBILLY beginnings to one of world's most popular soft drinks. Retrieved April 02, 2021, from https://www.southernthing.com/a-history-of-mountain-dew-from-hillbilly-beginnings-to-one-of-worlds-most-popular-soft-drinks-2646712730.html

Kiniry, L. (2016, August 16). The unusual origins of pink lemonade. Retrieved April 02, 2021, from https://www.smithsonianmag.com/history/unusual-origins-pink-lemonade-180960145/

Kirby's pig STAND. (2021, March 28). Retrieved April 05, 2021, from https://en.wikipedia.org/wiki/Kirby%27s_Pig_Stand

Leaf blower. (2021, February 08). Retrieved April 05, 2021, from https://en.wikipedia.org/wiki/Leaf_blower

Martin, C. (2015, August 15). EnChroma's accidental Spectacles find niche among the colorblind. Retrieved April 02, 2021, from https://www.nytimes.com/2015/08/16/business/enchromas-accidental-spectacles-find-niche-among-the-colorblind.html

McCarthy, A. (2016, October 20). A brief history of the SLURPEE, a Frozen American icon. Retrieved April 02, 2021, from https://www.eater.com/drinks/2016/10/20/13309514/slurpee-7-11-slushie-icee-history

McNamara, R. (n.d.). How edison invented the phonograph. Retrieved April 02, 2021, from https://www.thoughtco.com/invention-of-the-phonograph-4156528

Mikulec, T. (2019, November 12). The evolution of the gas pump. Retrieved April 05, 2021, from https://www.saferack.com/evolution-gas-pump/

Neo. (2018, January 23). Who discovered the first Synthetic Dye. Retrieved April 05, 2021, from https://www.whoinventedfirst.com/discovered-first-synthetic-dye/

Nix, E. (2015, February 13). Chew on this: The history of gum. Retrieved April 02, 2021, from https://www.history.com/news/chew-on-this-the-history-of-gum

NutraSweet company - company Profile, Information, business Description, history, background information On Nutrasweet company. (n.d.). Retrieved April 02, 2021, from https://www.referenceforbusiness.com/history2/7/NutraSweet-Company.html

Office of dietary supplements - phosphorus. (n.d.). Retrieved April 05, 2021, from https://ods.od.nih.gov/factsheets/Phosphorus-HealthProfessional/

Our heritage. (n.d.). Retrieved April 02, 2021, from https://ivory.com/our-heritage/

Our story. (n.d.). Retrieved April 02, 2021, from https://www.pepperidgefarm.com/our-story/

Patra, R. (2016, September 07). To dye for: A history of natural and synthetic dyes. Retrieved April 05, 2021, from https://blog.patra.com/2016/09/07/to-dye-for-a-history-of-natural-and-synthetic-dyes/

Penven, D. (n.d.). Cyanoacrylate fuming - a mainstay of crime Scene Investigation. Retrieved April 05, 2021, from https://www.crime-scene-investigator.net/cyanoacrylate-fuming-a-mainstay-of-crime-scene-investigation.html

Pepperidge farm. (2021, January 30). Retrieved April 02, 2021, from https://en.wikipedia.org/wiki/Pepperidge_Farm

Pepsi. (2021, March 30). Retrieved April 02, 2021, from https://en.wikipedia.org/wiki/Pepsi

Person. (n.d.). History of safety pins. Retrieved April 02, 2021, from https://fashion-history.lovetoknow.com/clothing-closures-embellishments/history-safety-pins

Phonograph. (2021, February 25). Retrieved April 02, 2021, from https://en.wikipedia.org/wiki/Phonograph

The phonograph. (n.d.). Retrieved April 02, 2021, from https://www.nps.gov/edis/learn/kidsyouth/the-phonograph.htm

Phosphorus. (2021, April 05). Retrieved April 05, 2021, from https://en.wikipedia.org/wiki/Phosphorus

Pitchfork. (2021, March 27). Retrieved April 05, 2021, from https://en.wikipedia.org/wiki/Pitchfork

Products. (n.d.). Retrieved April 05, 2021, from https://www.zout.com/products
Protective clothing - reflective clothing. (n.d.). Retrieved April 02, 2021, from https://oshwiki.eu/wiki/Protective_clothing_-_Reflective_clothing

A quick and fascinating history of smoke detectors. (2019, January 02). Retrieved April 02, 2021, from https://info.inspectpoint.com/smoke-detectors-history/

Rathburn, B. (2020, April 14). Wheaties were invented at this old, ABANDONED ruin In Minnesota from the 1800s. Retrieved April 02, 2021, from https://www.onlyinyourstate.com/minnesota/wheaties-invented-mn/

Saccharin. (2021, February 04). Retrieved April 02, 2021, from https://en.wikipedia.org/wiki/Saccharin

Sandwich. (n.d.). Retrieved April 02, 2021, from https://www.britannica.com/topic/sandwich

Schneider, S. (2018, January 17). Dry cleaning 101 & why it can be damaging. Retrieved April 02, 2021, from https://www.gentlemansgazette.com/dry-cleaning-101/

Scotchgard. (2021, March 07). Retrieved April 02, 2021, from https://en.wikipedia.org/wiki/Scotchgard
Scott, A. (2018, June 01). When did we discover fire? Here's what experts actually know. Retrieved April 05, 2021, from https://time.com/5295907/discover-fire/

Singh, I. (2020, April 26). Who invented the GPS? People behind the Global positioning system. Retrieved April 05, 2021, from https://geoawesomeness.com/who-invented-the-gps/

Sloppy joe. (2021, March 30). Retrieved April 02, 2021, from https://en.wikipedia.org/wiki/Sloppy_joe

Slurpee. (2021, February 20). Retrieved April 02, 2021, from https://en.wikipedia.org/wiki/Slurpee

Smith, K. (2018, August 01). Stronger than Steel: How Chemist Stephanie Kwolek Invented kevlar. Retrieved April 05, 2021, from https://www.forbes.com/sites/kionasmith/2018/07/31/stronger-than-steel-how-chemist-stephanie-kwolek-invented-kevlar/

Sodium cyclamate. (2021, February 13). Retrieved April 02, 2021, from https://en.wikipedia.org/wiki/Sodium_cyclamate

Spivey. (2013, April 23). How were smoke detectors invented? Retrieved April 02, 2021, from https://spiveyinsurancegroup.com/blog/how_were_smoke_detectors_invented/

Splenda. (2020, December 21). Retrieved April 02, 2021, from https://en.wikipedia.org/wiki/Splenda

Stephanie Kwolek. (2021, March 30). Retrieved April 05, 2021, from https://en.wikipedia.org/wiki/Stephanie_Kwolek

Stevens, T. (n.d.). The fascinating, MOONSHINE-INSPIRED origin story of Mountain Dew. Retrieved April 02, 2021, from https://www.myrecipes.com/community/mountain-dew-history

Stone, S. (2014, September 04). How dry cleaning works and who invented it. Retrieved April 02, 2021, from http://www.todayifoundout.com/index.php/2014/09/history-dry-cleaning/

Stradley, L. (2016, June 04). Iced tea history – sweet tea history. Retrieved April 02, 2021, from https://whatscookingamerica.net/History/IcedTeaHistory.htm

Stradley, L. (2016, June 04). Tarte TATIN history. Retrieved April 02, 2021, from https://whatscookingamerica.net/History/PieHistory/TarteTatin.htm

Stradley, L. (2019, May 14). Crepes Suzette history and recipe. Retrieved April 02, 2021, from https://whatscookingamerica.net/History/CrepesSuzetteHistory.htm

Stuber, C. (2021, January 14). 20 popular products that were originally intended for completely different uses. Retrieved April 05, 2021, from https://www.buzznicked.com/accidental-inventions/

The sugar Files archives. (n.d.). Retrieved April 02, 2021, from https://www.saveur.com/tags/sugar-files/
The surprising history of the discovery of superglue. (n.d.). Retrieved April 02, 2021, from https://gluereview.com/history-of-superglue/

Szczepanski, K. (n.d.). How China invented gunpowder. Retrieved April 05, 2021, from https://www.thoughtco.com/invention-of-gunpowder-195160

Tarte TATIN. (2020, November 07). Retrieved April 02, 2021, from https://en.wikipedia.org/wiki/Tarte_Tatin

Thomson, J. (2014, April 15). Why pink lemonade is pink. Retrieved April 02, 2021, from https://www.huffpost.com/entry/why-is-lemonade-pink_n_1503570

Toasted ravioli. (2020, December 08). Retrieved April 02, 2021, from https://en.wikipedia.org/wiki/Toasted_ravioli

Toasted ravioli. (n.d.). Retrieved April 02, 2021, from https://everipedia.org/wiki/lang_en/Toasted_ravioli

Tofu. (2021, March 26). Retrieved April 02, 2021, from https://en.wikipedia.org/wiki/Tofu

Tube (container). (2021, March 22). Retrieved April 05, 2021, from https://en.wikipedia.org/wiki/Tube_(container)

Uses of radiation I nrc.gov. (n.d.). Retrieved April 5, 2021, from https://www.nrc.gov/about-nrc/radiation/around-us/uses-radiation.html

VanHooker, B. (2020, November 09). The origins of the sloppy joe are as mysterious as its ingredients. Retrieved April 02, 2021, from https://melmagazine.com/en-us/story/sloppy-joe-history

Velcro. (2021, February 24). Retrieved April 05, 2021, from https://en.wikipedia.org/wiki/Velcro

Walter hunt (inventor). (2021, January 28). Retrieved April 02, 2021, from https://en.wikipedia.org/wiki/Walter_Hunt_(inventor)

What is A chimichanga? (n.d.). Retrieved April 02, 2021, from https://www.groupon.com/articles/what-is-a-chimichanga

What is yogurt? (2017, January 12). Retrieved April 02, 2021, from https://www.culturesforhealth.com/learn/yogurt/what-is-yogurt-history/

Wheaties. (2021, March 30). Retrieved April 02, 2021, from https://en.wikipedia.org/wiki/Wheaties

Wheaties. (n.d.). Retrieved April 02, 2021, from https://www.mnopedia.org/thing/wheaties

When Were Chainsaws Invented? (2020, April 08). Retrieved April 05, 2021, from https://chainsawlarry.com/when-were-chainsaws-invented/

Who invented the drive-thru window? (2021, March 01). Retrieved April 05, 2021, from https://www.letstakeacloserlook.com/2019/03/11/who-invented-the-drive-thru-window/

Who invented the smoke detector. (2014, June 27). Retrieved April 02, 2021, from https://visionlaunch.com/who-invented-the-smoke-detector/

Who invented toasted ravioli? (2015, November 20). Retrieved April 02, 2021, from https://www.stlmag.com/news/who-invented-toasted-ravioli/

Why all pitchforks are not alike. (n.d.). Retrieved April 05, 2021, from https://www.farmcollector.com/steam-traction/why-all-pitchforks-are-not-alike

Worcestershire sauce. (2021, March 24). Retrieved April 02, 2021, from https://en.wikipedia.org/wiki/Worcestershire_sauce

Yogurt. (2021, March 08). Retrieved April 02, 2021, from https://en.wikipedia.org/wiki/Yogurt

Zhou, L. (2015, March 03). A scientist accidentally developed sunglasses that could correct color blindness. Retrieved April 02, 2021, from https://www.smithsonianmag.com/innovation/scientist-accidentally-developed-sunglasses-that-could-correct-color-blindness-180954456/

Made in the USA
Middletown, DE
17 November 2022

15320818R00077